AF426023

Here's what people are saying about
Everything You Never Wanted to Know About Color...

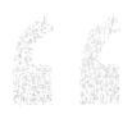 I Loved, Loved the Book! Janie really knows her Colors!

Everything You Never Wanted to Know About Color: A Guide to Color-Confidence in Your Brand & More is a wonderful book for any entrepreneur looking to create a company logo or develop their next marketing piece.

The first few chapters were fun, learning about color theory and the color wheel. Then discovering the difference between RGB and CMYK and that colors carry emotional feelings. Who Knew?

My favorite graphic is on page 68 where Janie shows the colors of popular brands and the messages and feelings associated with each company. Now I know WHY she challenged me so much when I was choosing the colors of my company brand. Colors Really Do Matter!!"

Pat Batchelor, PE
Owner/President
Engineering Search Partners, Inc.

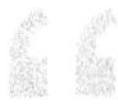 *Everything You Never Wanted to Know About Color: A Guide to Color-Confidence in Your Brand & More* is a great book for both beginners and seasoned graphic designers. The ideas are put forth in a logical order and are easy to understand. Sometimes, as seasoned designers, we know what works but don't always know the reason behind what we do. This book helps to give that reasoning and more depth to our knowledge to better put it into practice."

Richard Price
Owner/Lead Designer
PTGXtreme

" Despite spending more than 40 years in graphic arts, and even teaching it at a university, I was surprised at the quantity of things I learned in this book! *Everything You Never Wanted to Know About Color* is surprisingly rich in information with in-depth coverage of color and its application in visual media. Every person in print or electronic media would do themselves a favor by digging into this virtual information warehouse. If you're an entrepreneur planning on a new company, product, or brand, this invaluable reference will definitely give you a leg up on the competition."

John Owen
Renowned Artist, Graphic Designer, Former Professor and Janie's Uncle (her dad's brother)

" There is more to color than what meets the eye. And if you've never thought about that, you will after reading this book. In this beautiful, explicative, and playful book, Janie unlocks the mystery and mystique of how colors influence perceptions, touch emotions, and sway decisions. Whether you are trying to decide on brand colors in your business, remodeling your home, or finding the perfect attire for a special occasion, you'll discover how color matters."

Annette Bridges
Cattle rancher, magazine columnist, gift shop owner (and a client who has worked with Janie for over a decade on numerous business and personal projects)
Ranch House Press

" Are you starting out in a design career? Or do you just want to learn more about which colors work well together and which don't? Janie Owen-Bugh's *Everything You Never Wanted to Know About Color: A Guide to Color-Confidence in Your Brand & More* is the book for you. Janie is a seasoned graphic designer with decades of experience and a family background in printing. This latest book makes color theory interesting and accessible. Plus, the book includes discussions of well-known company color schemes and why they work so you can learn by example. This book is an enjoyable read, with gorgeous illustrations. If you're at all interested in learning more about color, I highly recommend this book."

Laura Spencer
Writer/Editor

JANIE OWEN-BUGH

EVERYTHING YOU NEVER WANTED TO KNOW ABOUT COLOR

A Guide to Color-Confidence in Your Brand & More

This book contains images of logos and trademarks that are the property
of their respective owners. These images are used for educational purposes
only and are not intended to infringe on the copyright of any owner.

AI (Artificial Intellegence) was minimally used in this book. Midjourney was used in two illustrations
(page 22 and page 60); and ChatGPT was used to summarize the positive, negative, and cultural
effects of the colors in *Chapter 7: The Good, The Bad, and The Different* and also used to help generate
the glossary. However, both were edited by humans.

Copyright © 2024, Janie Owen-Bugh

All Rights Reserved. No part of this book may be used or reproduced in any manner without the
prior written permission of the author except for the use of brief quotations in a book review.

To request permissions, contact the author at author@janieowenbugh.com

ISBN: 979-8-9896731-1-7

Cover art, layout and illustrations by Janie Owen-Bugh unless otherwise credited
Cover image painted by Peter Walkabout (a.k.a. Pete Owen)

Stock art and images licensed through Adobe Stock. No responsibility is accepted by author, producer,
publisher, or printer for any infringement of copyright, or otherwise, arising from the contents of this
publication. Every effort has been made to ensure that credits accurately comply with information
supplied. Contact author@janieowenbugh.com if you have any questions or concerns.

Published under the imprint

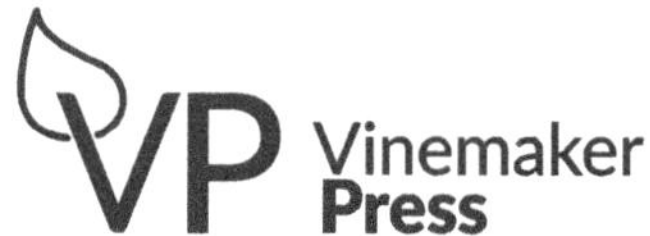

Printed in the USA.

Dedication

I'm dedicating this book to my clients. Without
their frustrations and confusion over color,
I would not have been inspired to write it.

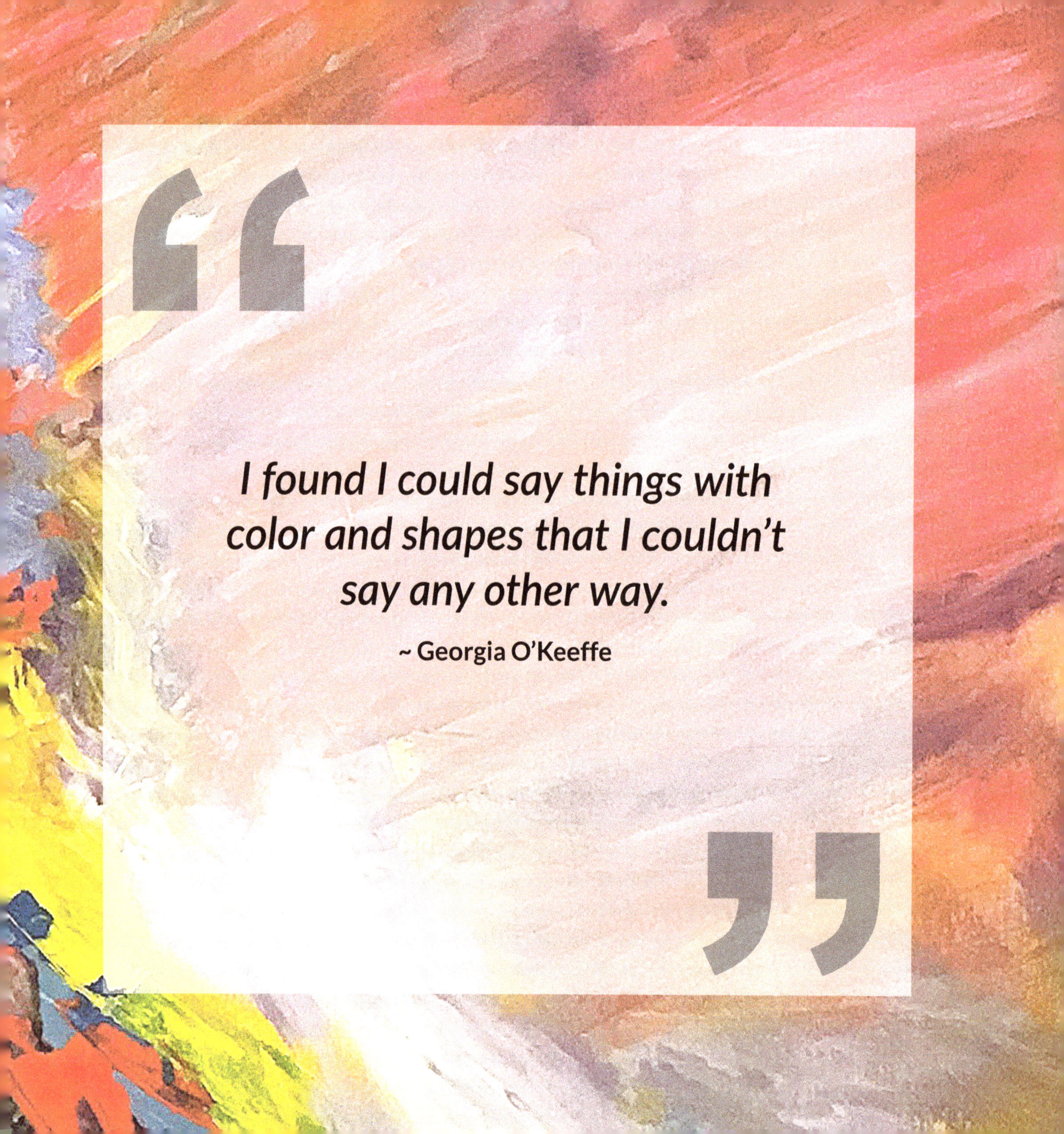

I found I could say things with color and shapes that I couldn't say any other way.
~ Georgia O'Keeffe

Table of Contents

Part 1
Understanding How Color Works (Color Basics)

Appendix

Understanding the Meaning of Color

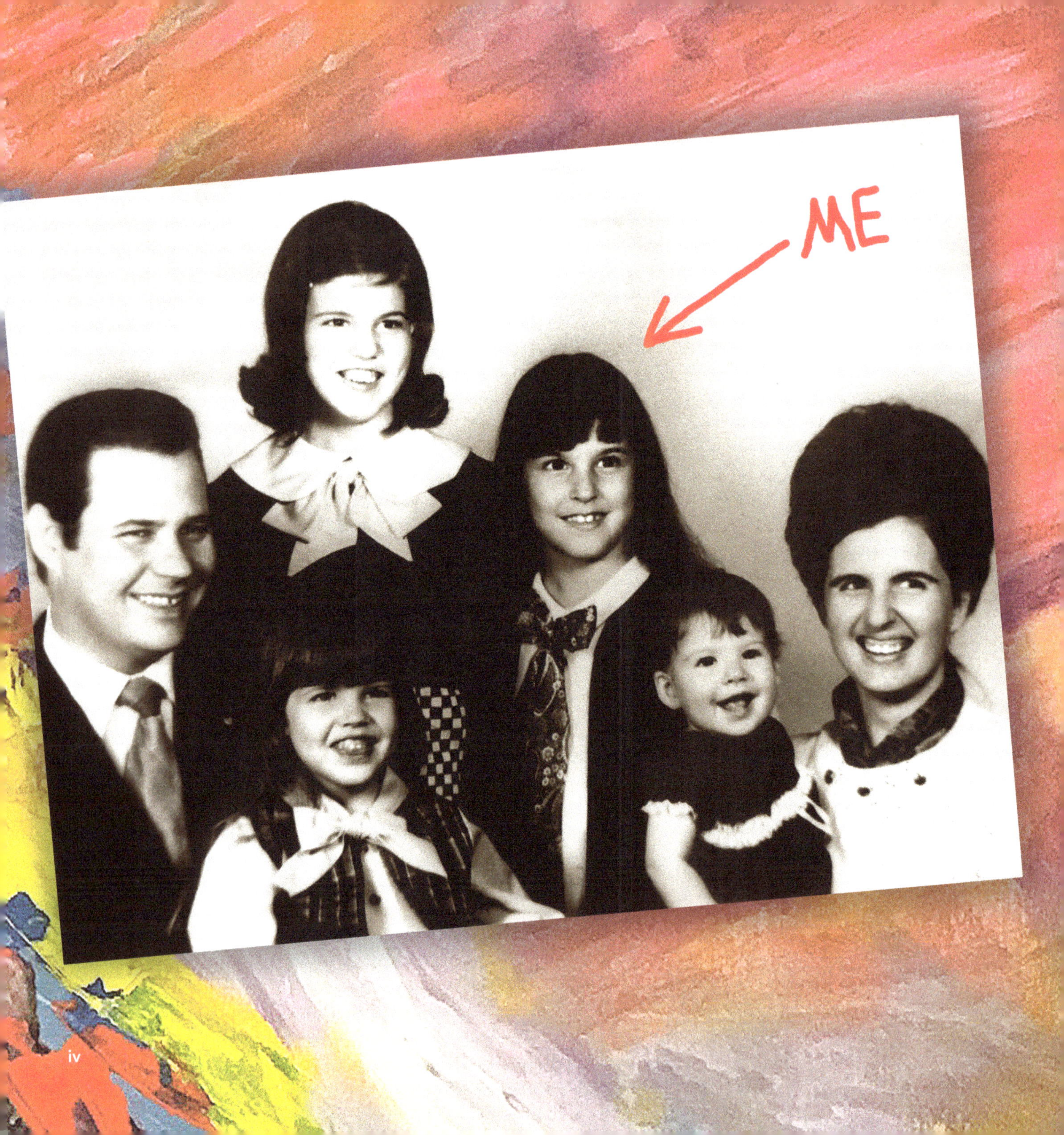

ME

Preface

I always say that I grew up in a print shop. Though it's not entirely true, it feels like it. Before owning his first printing company, my dad sold commercial cameras and supplies to large commercial printers and worked as a pressman. I loved spending time in his print shops. I remember when one of his clients was running for office—city council, I think. My dad handled all his campaign materials—yard signs, banners, flyers, postcards, and even "Vote for Me" pins. This was when I first became intrigued by graphics.

My dad was a pretty decent graphic designer, though I never heard him refer to himself as such. He was also an award-winning amateur photographer, so we always had a darkroom somewhere in our house—the garage, the bathroom—and now at his shop. This is when I first discovered silk-screening (a form of printing used to make T-shirts and other promotional materials like... yard signs), which required a darkroom. I was mesmerized by my dad in the darkroom as he developed photos and now as he "burned" the screens for silk-screening. I got to squeegee the ink across the screen to make the yard signs. It took me a few tries to get it right, but I loved it!

Fast forward a few years to when I was in high school. My mom, who had always been my dad's bookkeeper, joined him full-time on the premises. My three sisters and I were expected to help out. One job we were often asked to do was to walk in a circle around a big worktable with stacks of printed pages for a book, picking up one page at a time to collate them together to be bound. At this point, I hated working there, especially since it meant missing out on other extra-curricular activities. I was a teenager, so what did you expect? I vowed never to be in the graphics business.

Instead, I decided to be an architect. I was good at it, too. I was one of two girls in my drafting class (the other girl in my class actually went on to become a successful architect), and I won an award or two with my designs and a Who's Who in Industrial Arts. I also received a college scholarship. Soon after my first semester of college started, however, I found out I was pregnant. So, long story short, life went a different direction. My mom suggested I go into graphic design, so I took an Advertising Layout class at the local community college. I was hooked! I went on to work as a production artist, layout artist, graphic designer, and art director for various companies, and yes, a few printing companies, before deciding to freelance.

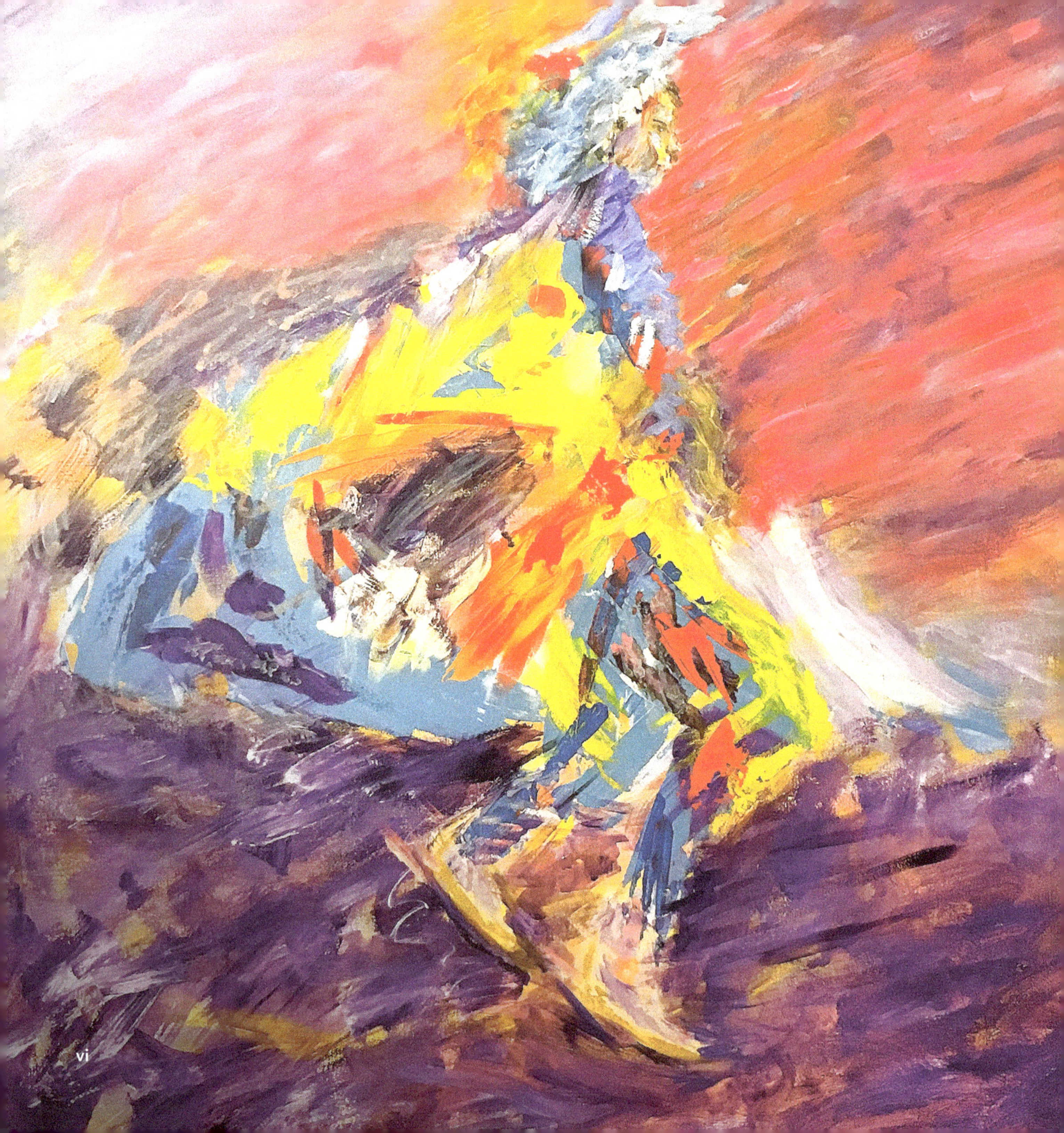

As a freelancer, I found myself with clients who needed printing done, so, of course, I brought the work to my dad. He was a craftsman... a perfectionist. He was constantly fixing the art his customers brought him, but did he fix mine? Nope. He would give it back and say, "You know that I have to run this job on the AB Dick. So, you know that I'm going to need more gutter than that." Then, I'd have to fix it myself.

Did I tell you about topics at the dinner table? He would hand me a loupe (small magnifying glass) and a brochure and ask me how many colors were there. I'd look at it and say with pride and certainty, knowing that he hadn't fooled me, that it had five colors. Because, in addition to the four colors in four-color process, there was a spot varnish. He'd look at me, shake his head, and say, "Try again." That's when I could see not only an additional varnish but also a solid Pantone color. It had seven colors! So embarrassing, but I learned.

My dad passed away over twenty years ago and still, to this day, I remember the lessons he

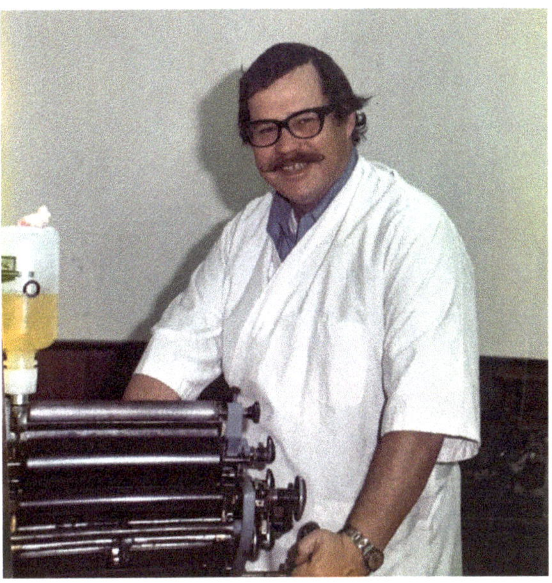

My Dad and his AB Dick printing press (circa 1975)

taught me. He has been the biggest influence on my career. For years after he passed, I would find myself picking up the phone to call him for advice on a project I was working on, only to realize he wasn't there. I still miss him. Since his passing, my mom (who has been there for me my entire life, though I haven't always wanted to admit it) and I have become very close. I couldn't do life without her.

I hope you can use this book to gain some of the knowledge that I've learned over my life and career to advance your business to the next level, or to better understand what color can do for you.

Later in life, my dad became an abstract painter. This one, "Fancy Dancer," is my favorite. It took many years after my dad's passing for my mom to part with it. It was a perfect birthday gift. I love his deliberate, yet random, strokes of color that portray movement and beauty all at once. I remember standing in the lobby of my parent's printing company, admiring it as it hung on the wall. He stood by me and told me that he had painted most of it weeks prior, but it didn't look finished. Then, he put a White dot in the eye of the dancer to reflect the fire, and it was done. Sometimes, it's the little things that make the biggest impact.

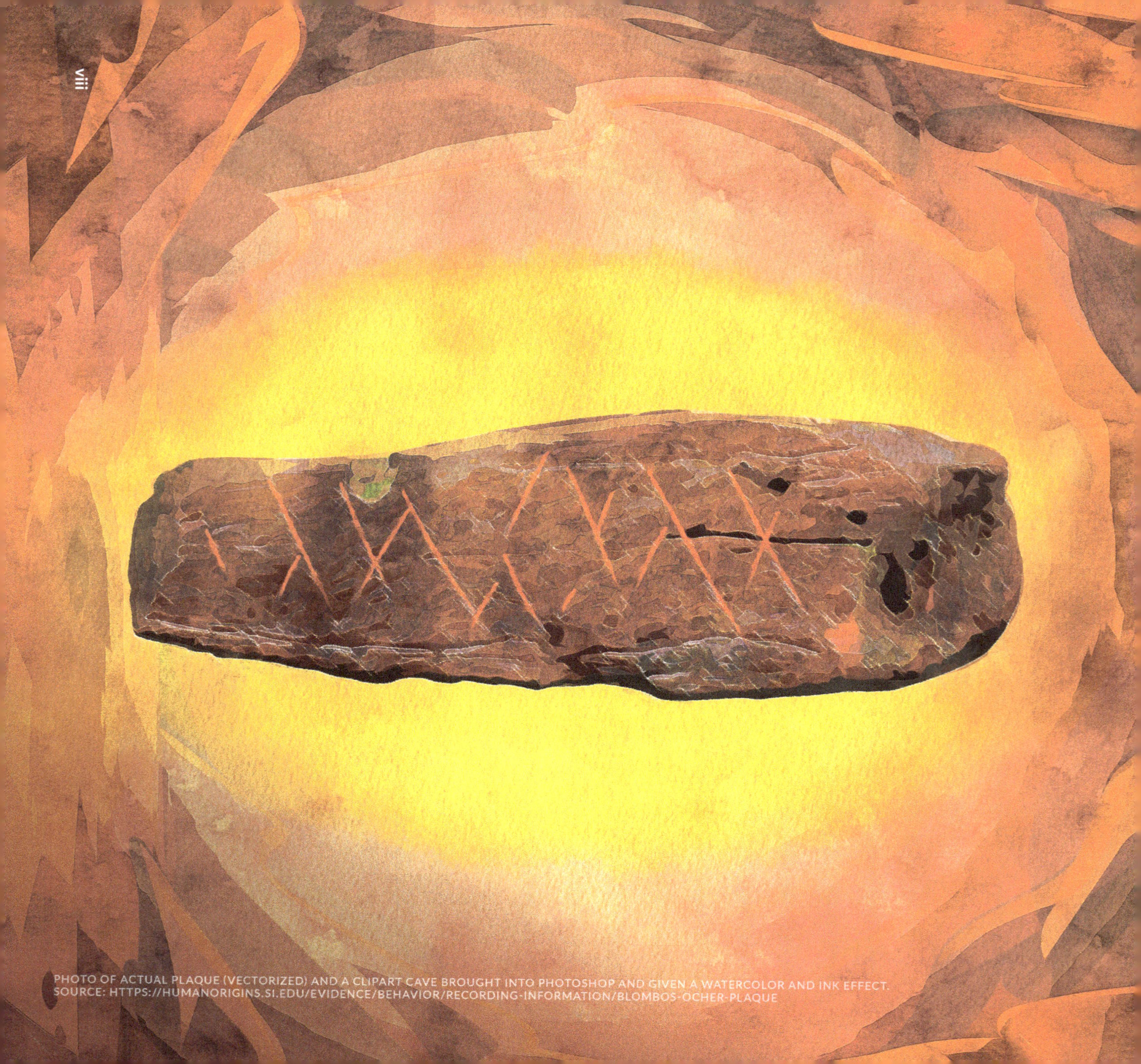

PHOTO OF ACTUAL PLAQUE (VECTORIZED) AND A CLIPART CAVE BROUGHT INTO PHOTOSHOP AND GIVEN A WATERCOLOR AND INK EFFECT.
SOURCE: HTTPS://HUMANORIGINS.SI.EDU/EVIDENCE/BEHAVIOR/RECORDING-INFORMATION/BLOMBOS-OCHER-PLAQUE

Introduction

When I set out to write this book, I wanted it to be easy to understand and as accurate as possible. In my research, I discovered many discrepancies in the world of color theory. So, I'm making a disclaimer right up front. I don't claim to be all-knowing by any stretch of the imagination, but I have unlearned and relearned some information that I had forgotten or just had all wrong. I'm passing that knowledge on to you.

How to Use This Guide

Throughout this book, I will share fun facts about color. For instance...

Fun Fact: The first color ever used as an art medium was Red—from ochre. An over 75,000-year-old Red ochre plaque was found in Blombos Cave in South Africa not too long ago, with symbolic engravings of triangles, lines, and diamond shapes.

I have also included lots of graphics to help you understand the color concepts presented. I hope that, along with resources and a glossary section at the end, will encourage you to refer to this book often when deciding what color to use in your brand, décor, wardrobe, or even the car you drive.

The Origins of Colors

First, we will discover or rediscover the color wheel (Part 1: *Understanding How Color Works [Color Basics]*) and explore a simplified version of color theory by looking at color schemes and how they help to harmonize color relationships.

Seeing Colors

Did you know that light's reflection determines how we see color? Light reflects differently with each color, Whether on a flat surface or through a TV screen. We'll discuss that in Part 2: *Understanding How We See Color (Color Systems)*.

Choosing Colors

Sometimes, when we choose a color, we might decide on a whim, like "Let's paint that wall Yellow," "Let's buy a Black table," or "Blue curtains would look good in here." Or maybe we agonize over the decision and bring a

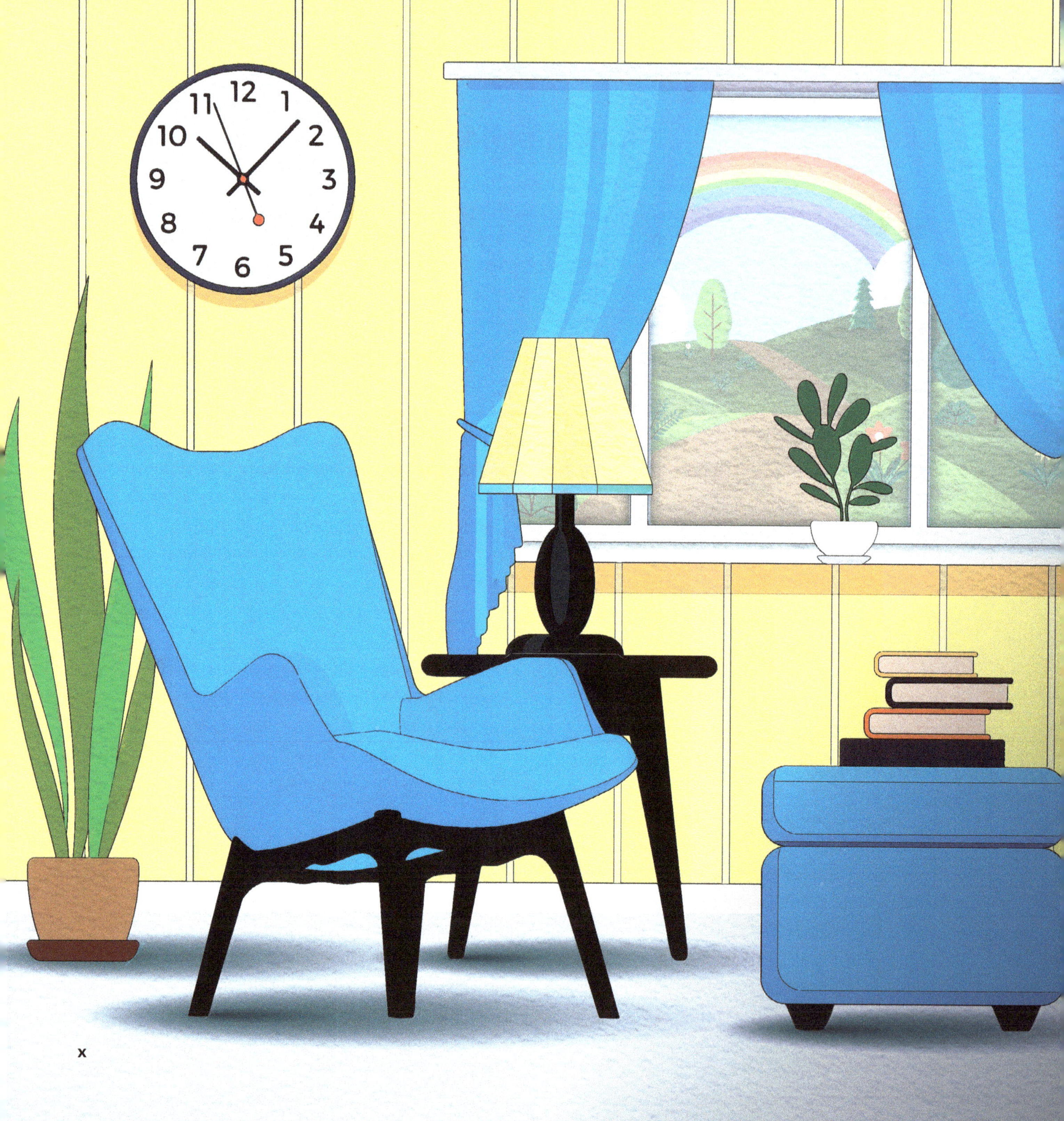

multitude of swatches or samples home from the paint store to see how it would look.

———

Fun Fact: Blue is the most common favorite color in the world. Several global marketing firms have conducted studies showing that Blue is the most popular color, followed by Purple. What's your favorite color? Mine is Green.

———

But do you know that there is a subconscious decision behind every color choice? Why did you buy the Yellow soap instead of the White one? Why did you buy that specific shirt or blouse? Why do you see a dominant color in your closet? You try to buy different colors but always end up with one color more than all the others.

There is a deep meaning and identity behind each color and color combination. We, as humans, are wired to act according to them. We will explore the emotions of color in Part 3: *Understanding How Color Makes Us Feel (Color Psychology)*.

Colors have so much importance in our lives that even a lot of scientists and some of the greatest thinkers were consumed by them. In fact, the German writer and scientist Goethe thought his study *"Theory of Colors"* was the most important of all his works.

Using Colors in Business

Why am I telling you all this? Because in my line of work, color is everything. As a graphic designer, I always work with colors, whether I am creating a logo, a banner, a website, a brochure, or anything in between.

If my clients had one common struggle over the years, it would be a lack of confidence and understanding in using color. I want to make it easier for color-challenged entrepreneurs (and others) so that they can fully understand the implications of selecting specific brand colors for their logo, website, business stationery, and everything else. I hope you find this guide a helpful resource. Now, let's get started.

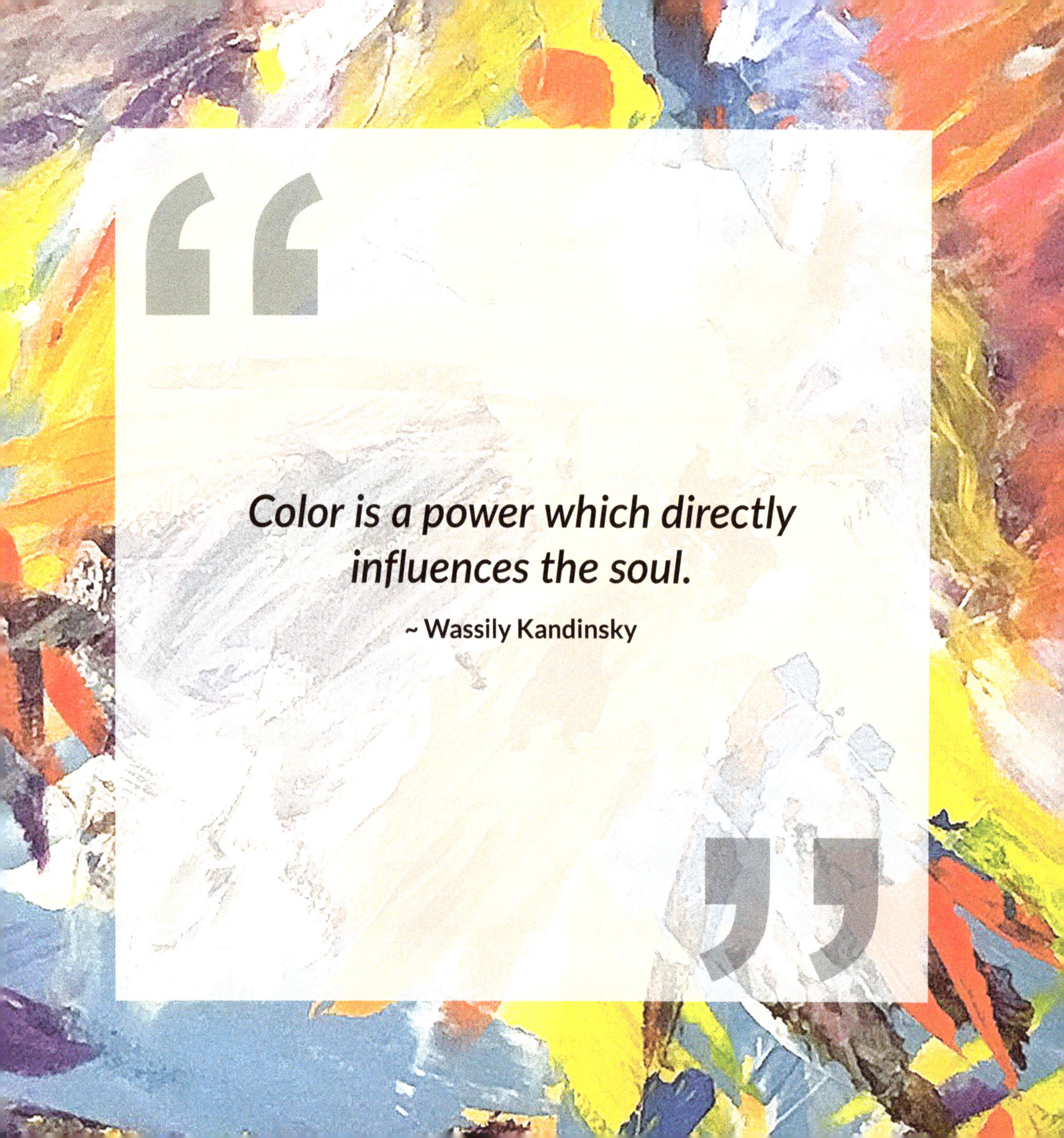
Color is a power which directly influences the soul.
~ Wassily Kandinsky

PART 1: UNDERSTANDING HOW COLOR WORKS

[COLOR BASICS]

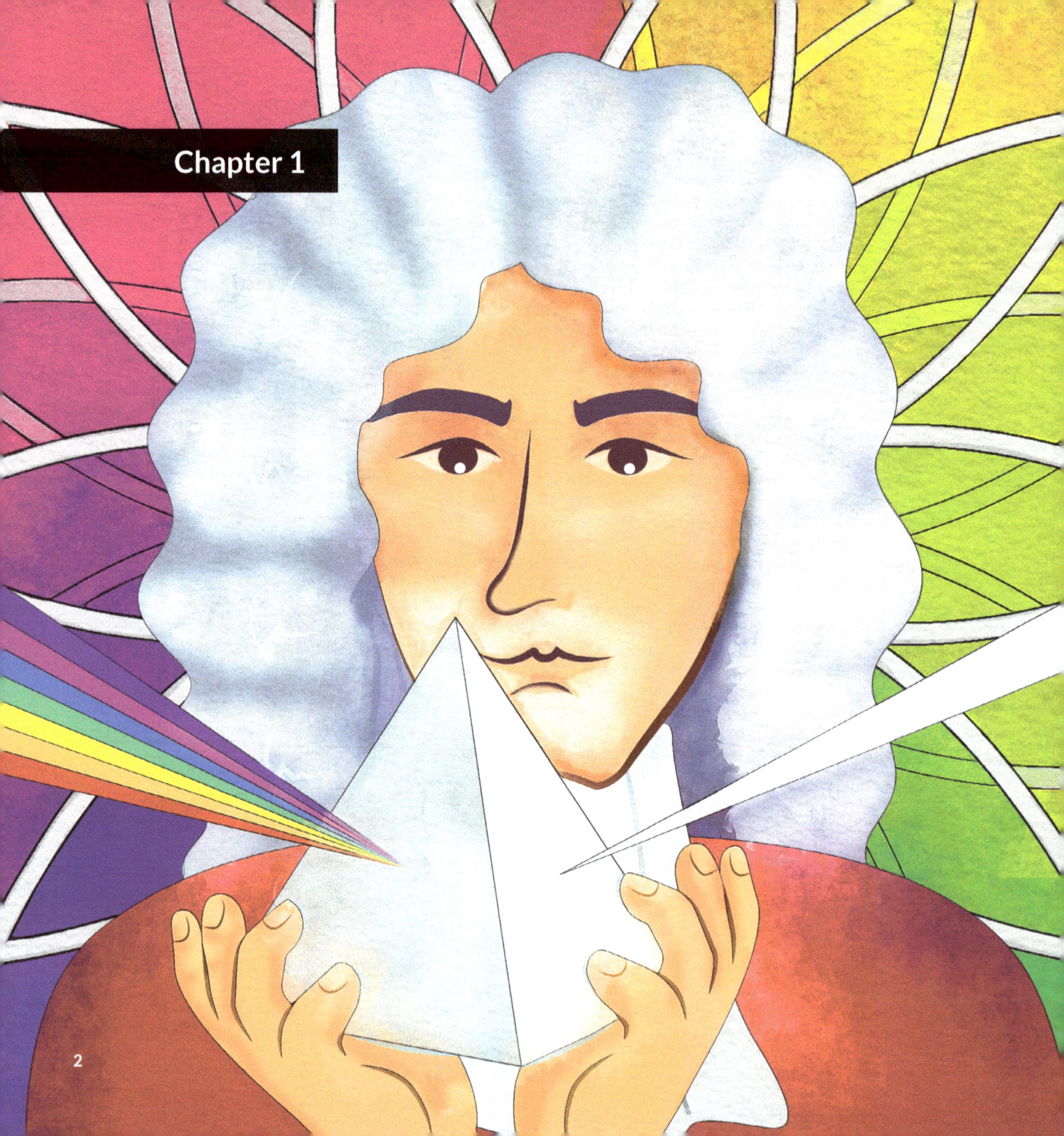
Chapter 1

The Color Wheel Is How We Roll

Do you remember the feeling you got back when you were a kid with a box of crayons? I always looked forward to the first day of school each year because I would get a brand-new box of colored pencils, crayons, or both. It was an eight-count box for school, but I had a 64-count box at home. It even came with a crayon sharpener! I loved the many shades of Green, Blue, Yellow, and even Black. There were a million possibilities I could explore with color. Understanding the color wheel and its intricacies can be just as exciting as receiving a brand-new box of crayons!

You will improve your communication once you understand color and when to use it. You can work with your graphic designer, web designer, or printer and know what they mean when they ask about your colors. Better yet, learning about color will equip you to tell a striking visual—and colorful—story. So, let's get right down to it.

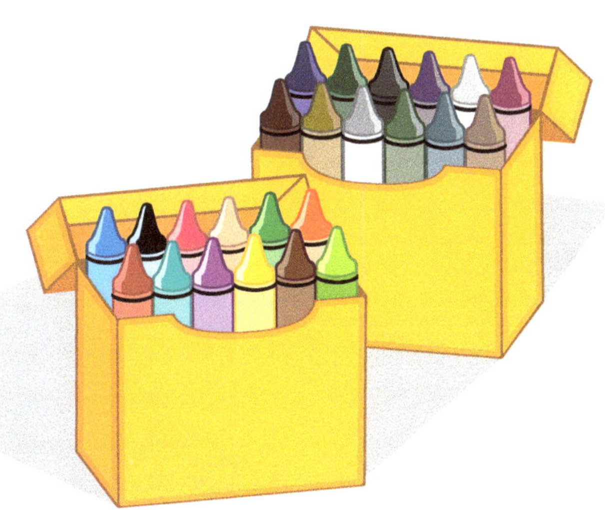

Who's Roy G. Biv?

Sir Isaac Newton first designed the color wheel in the 17th century. Believe it or not, at the time, there was a pandemic—the bubonic plague. Isolated, he had nothing better to do than to study color and how it worked. He was the first to determine that various colors made White light. In other words, colors of light all shining together create White light. Remember that when we get to Part 2. He noticed the colors of a prism always refracted the same set of colors that you would see in a rainbow. For example, raindrops are a bunch of prisms, so that's how we get the rainbow. Newton, back then, defined the order of the colors for the rainbow. In art class, we had an acronym: ROY G BIV (Red– Orange–Yellow, Green, Blue–Indigo–Violet). I will come back to this in a little bit. But first, let's take a closer look at the color wheel.

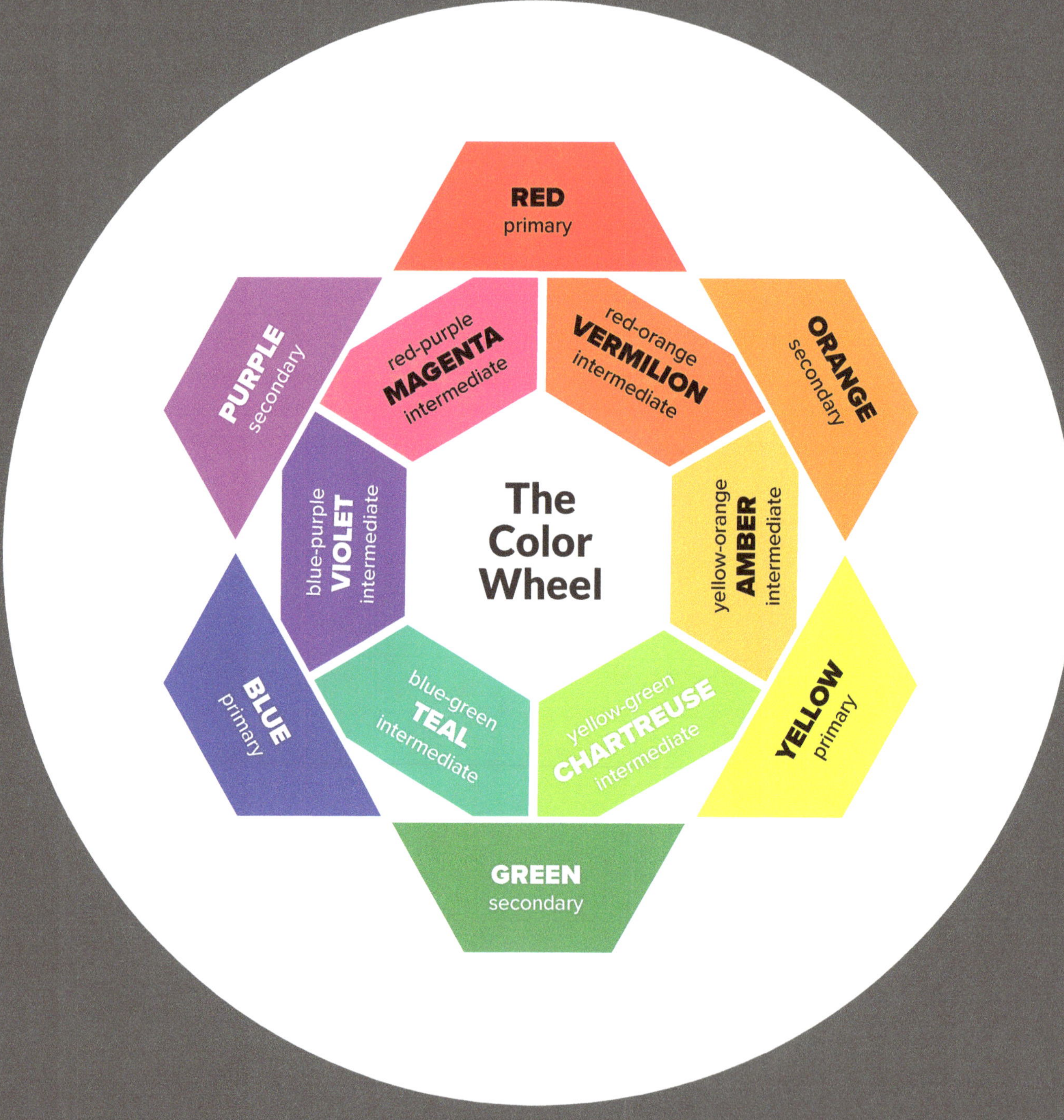

The Color Wheel

RED
primary

red-purple
MAGENTA
intermediate

red-orange
VERMILION
intermediate

ORANGE
secondary

PURPLE
secondary

blue-purple
VIOLET
intermediate

yellow-orange
AMBER
intermediate

BLUE
primary

blue-green
TEAL
intermediate

yellow-green
CHARTREUSE
intermediate

YELLOW
primary

GREEN
secondary

The Color Wheel

Before we get started, I want to explain a few things. The color wheel depicted in this book is my version of the original color wheel. There are a lot of versions out there. They each have slight differences, but the basics are the same. Also, the theories we discuss here work across color systems. We talk about color systems in Part 2. The following information may seem incorrect if you are already familiar with CMYK or RGB color models. Please bear with me; I will show you how you can universally apply the concepts in this book.

In the following pages, we will dissect this Isaac Newton-inspired version of the color wheel. I will use the analogy of a family to help it to make sense. Understanding how color works starts with understanding the origins of colors and how they came to be.

A parent analogy illustrates the connections between the colors on the color wheel. Later, in Chapter 2, we will explore the relationships that colors have with each other via color schemes.

Introducing the Crayons—a colorful family. Let's have some fun.

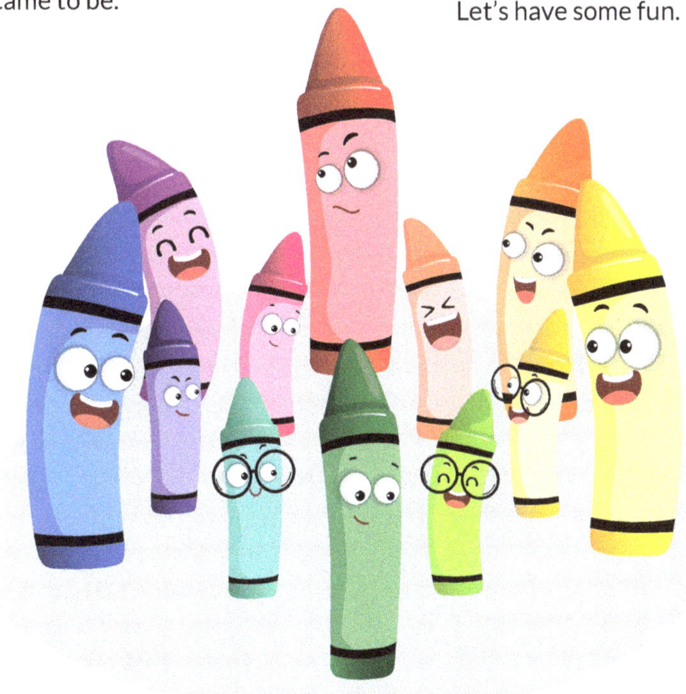

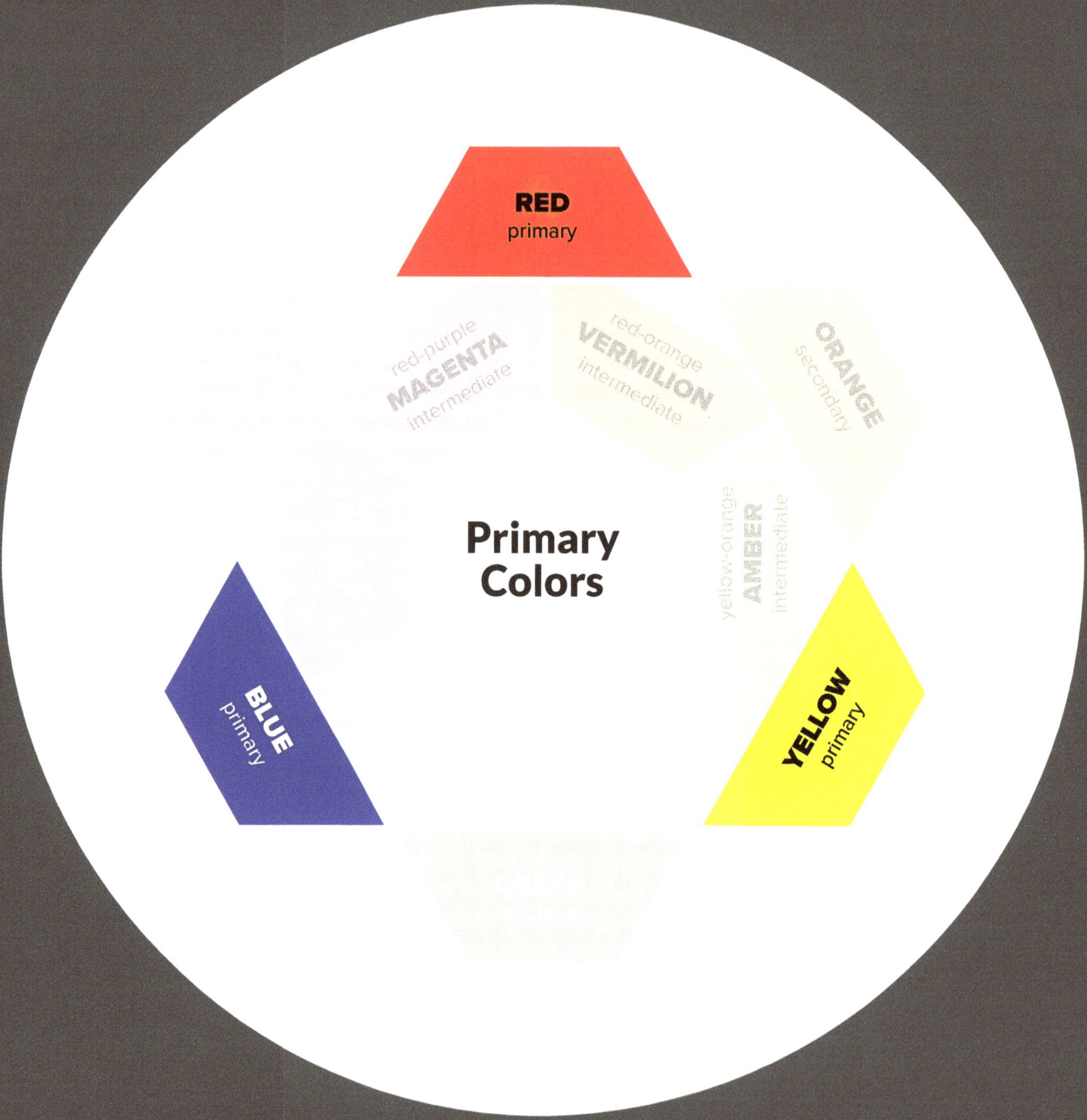

RED
primary
red-purple
MAGENTA
intermediate
red-orange
VERMILION
intermediate
ORANGE
secondary
yellow-orange
AMBER
intermediate
Primary
Colors
BLUE
primary
YELLOW
primary

The Parents
Primary Colors (The Originals)

To start, our family has three primary colors: Red, Yellow, and Blue. These are the parents of all colors—the pure colors. Mixing these three primary colors together, along with Black and White, will make just about any other color you can imagine. These colors are considered pure hues (hue is another word for color) or the only colors that cannot be created by mixing other colors. In our Crayon family, they are the parents.

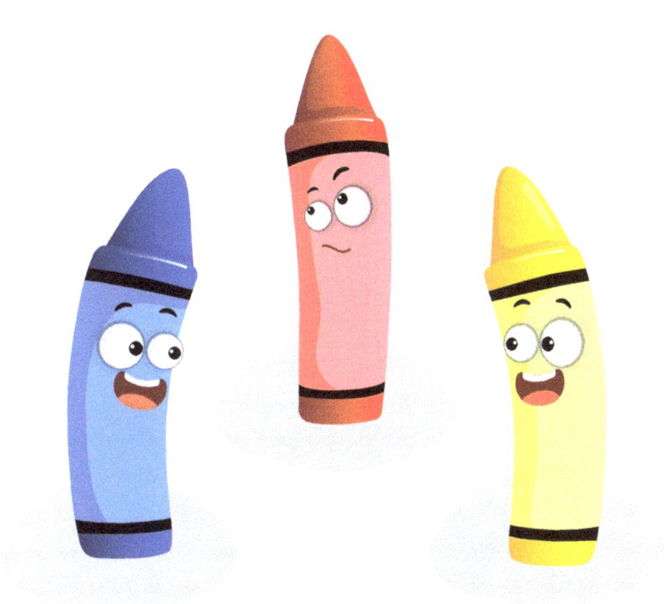

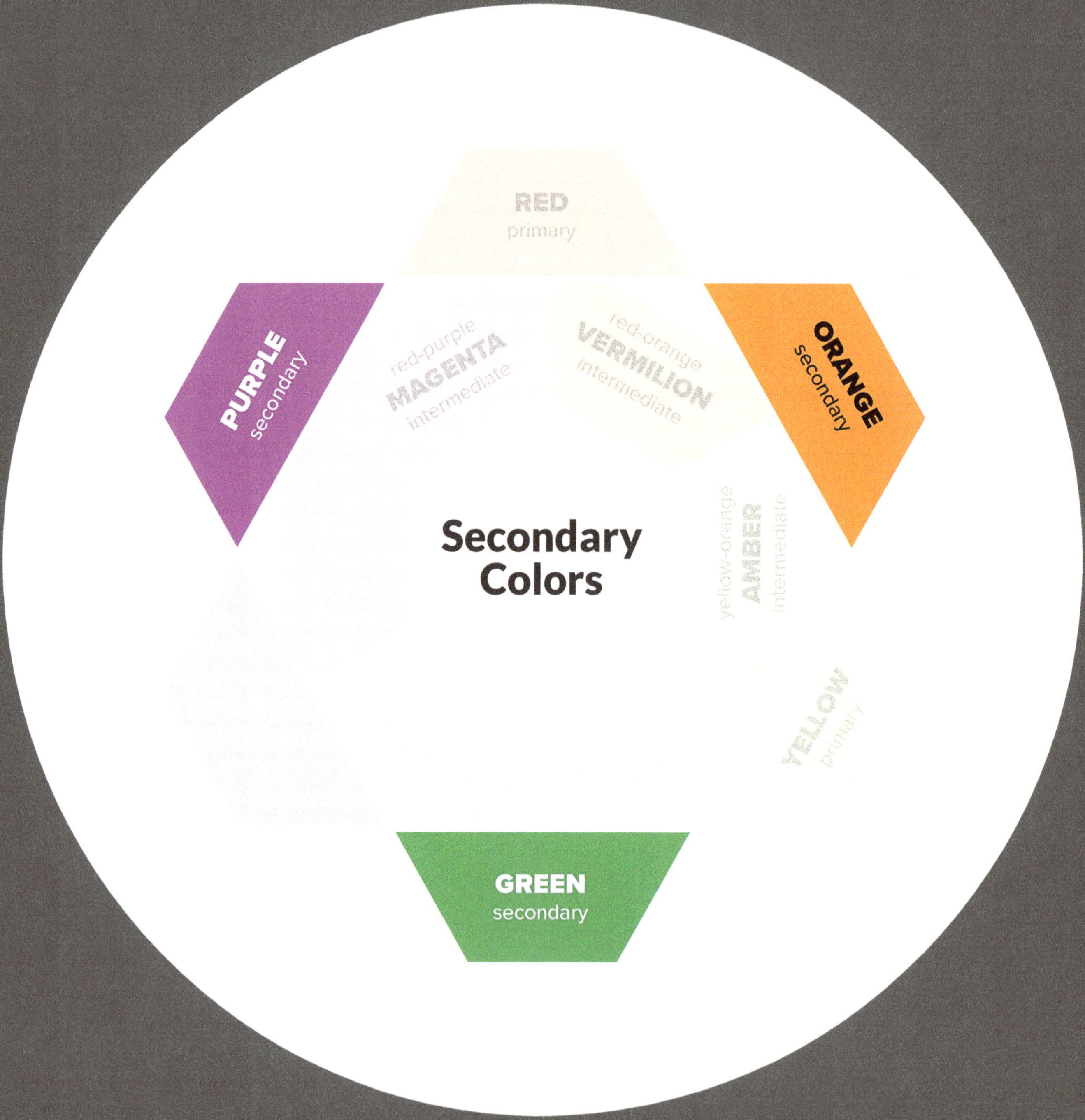

RED
primary
PURPLE
secondary
red-purple
MAGENTA
intermediate
red-orange
VERMILION
intermediate
ORANGE
secondary
Secondary
Colors
yellow-orange
AMBER
intermediate
YELLOW
primary
GREEN
secondary

The Children
Secondary Colors (Born from Primaries)

Then we have the three secondary colors. These are colors that we create by equally mixing the primary colors, their parent colors. These are Green, Orange, and Purple. Orange is the child of Red and Yellow. Green is made with Yellow and Blue. Purple is created from Blue and Red.

Fun Fact: *Some people like to include Green as a primary because it's somewhat different from the other secondary colors. Orange is similar to Red and Yellow, and Purple is similar to Blue and Red. However, Blue and Yellow create a color that seems a bit more different. You can mix all three primaries to make Brown or Black. So, it stands to reason that you can also use Green and Red.*

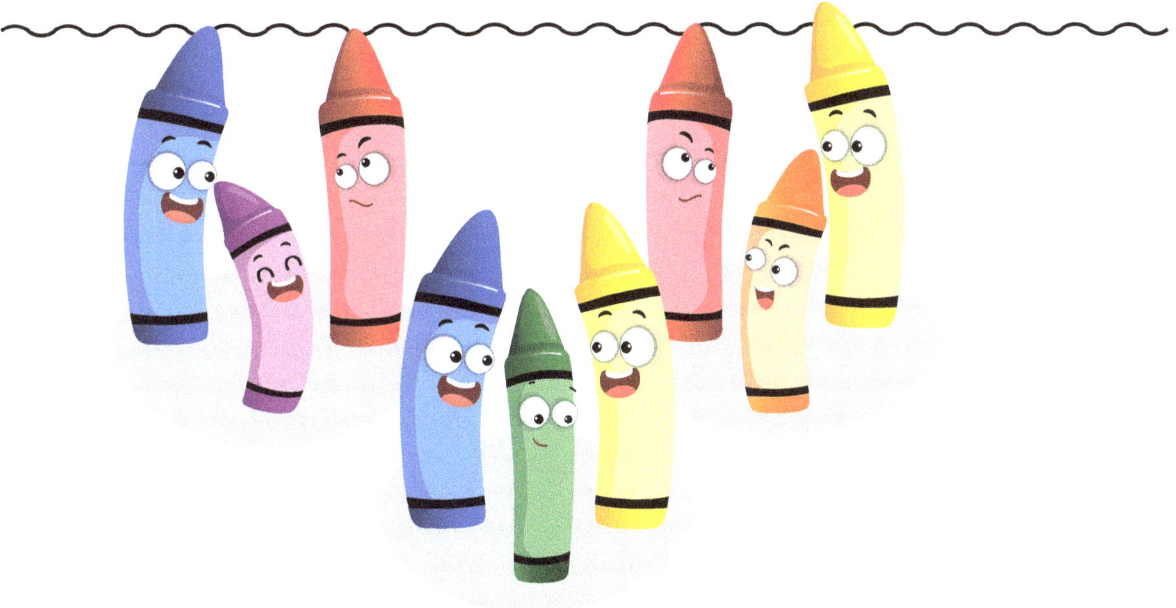

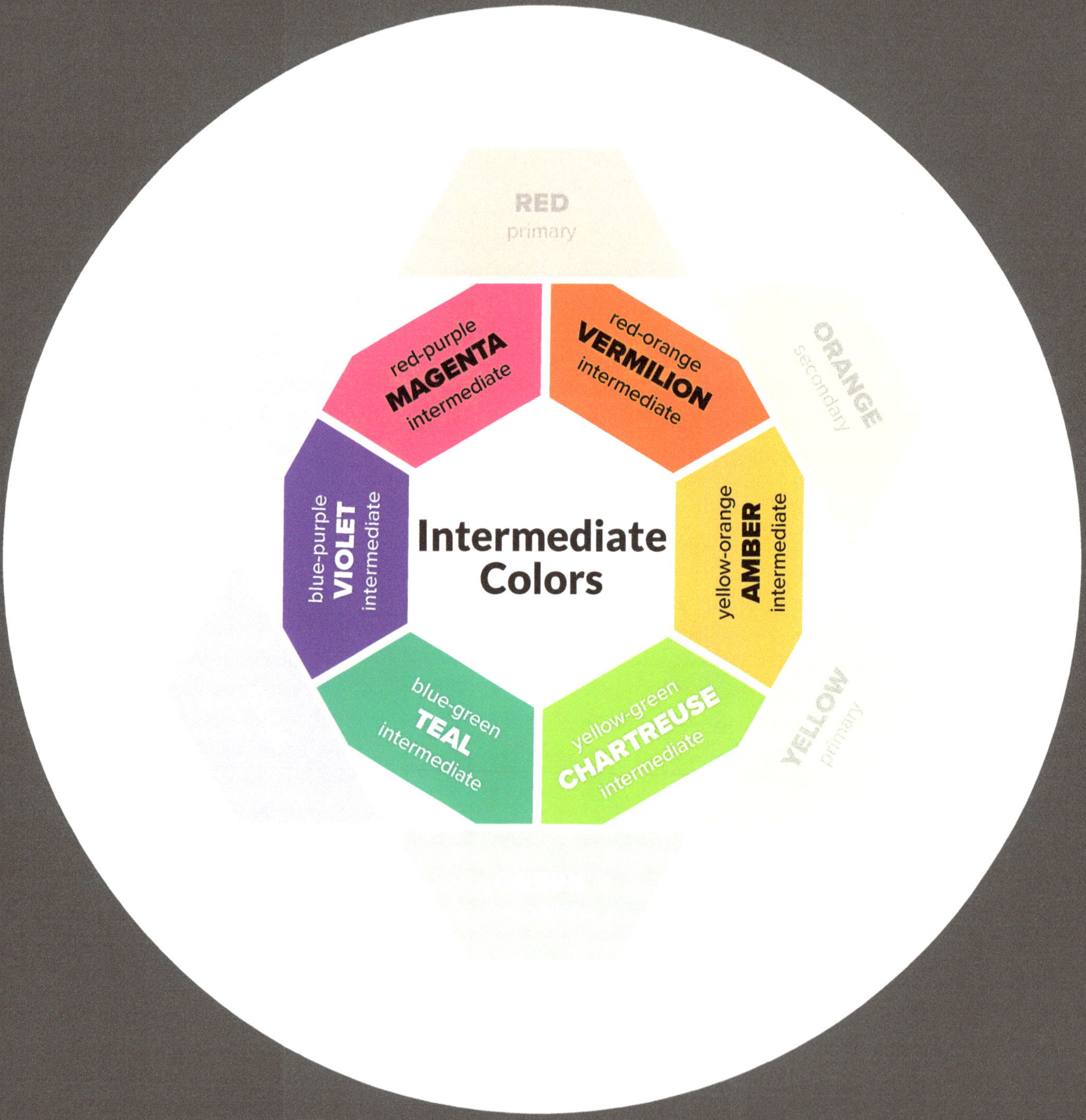

RED
primary
ORANGE
secondary
YELLOW
primary
Intermediate Colors
red-purple
MAGENTA
intermediate
red-orange
VERMILION
intermediate
blue-purple
VIOLET
intermediate
yellow-orange
AMBER
intermediate
blue-green
TEAL
intermediate
yellow-green
CHARTREUSE
intermediate

The Problem Children
Intermediates (Born from a Primary and a Secondary)

Lastly, the color wheel shows us six intermediate colors (often referred to as tertiary colors). These colors are made by mixing equal amounts of the adjacent primary and secondary colors. The parent analogy here is... well, it gets complicated. Its parents are a primary and a second-ary, which means one of its parents is also a grandparent.

The official names of intermediate colors are Red-Orange, Yellow-Orange, Yellow-Green, Blue-Green, Blue-Purple, and Red-Purple. Note that the primary color is always listed first in these compound-word names.

Their nicknames vary, but the ones portrayed on my color wheel are the names I've always referred to them as Vermilion, Amber, Chartreuse, Teal, Violet, and Magenta.

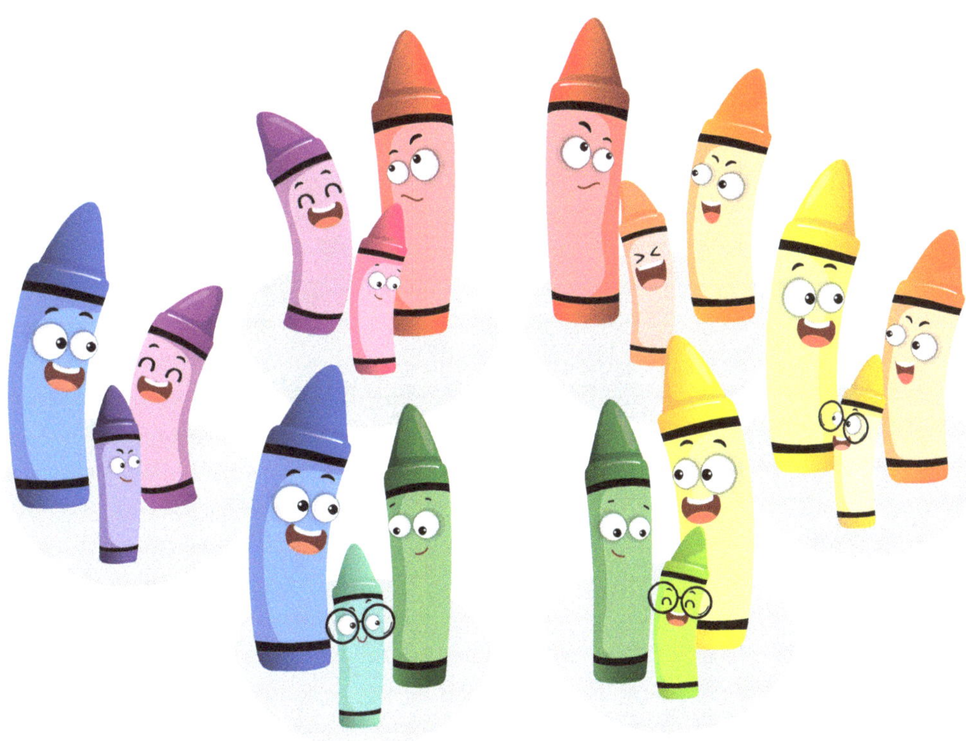

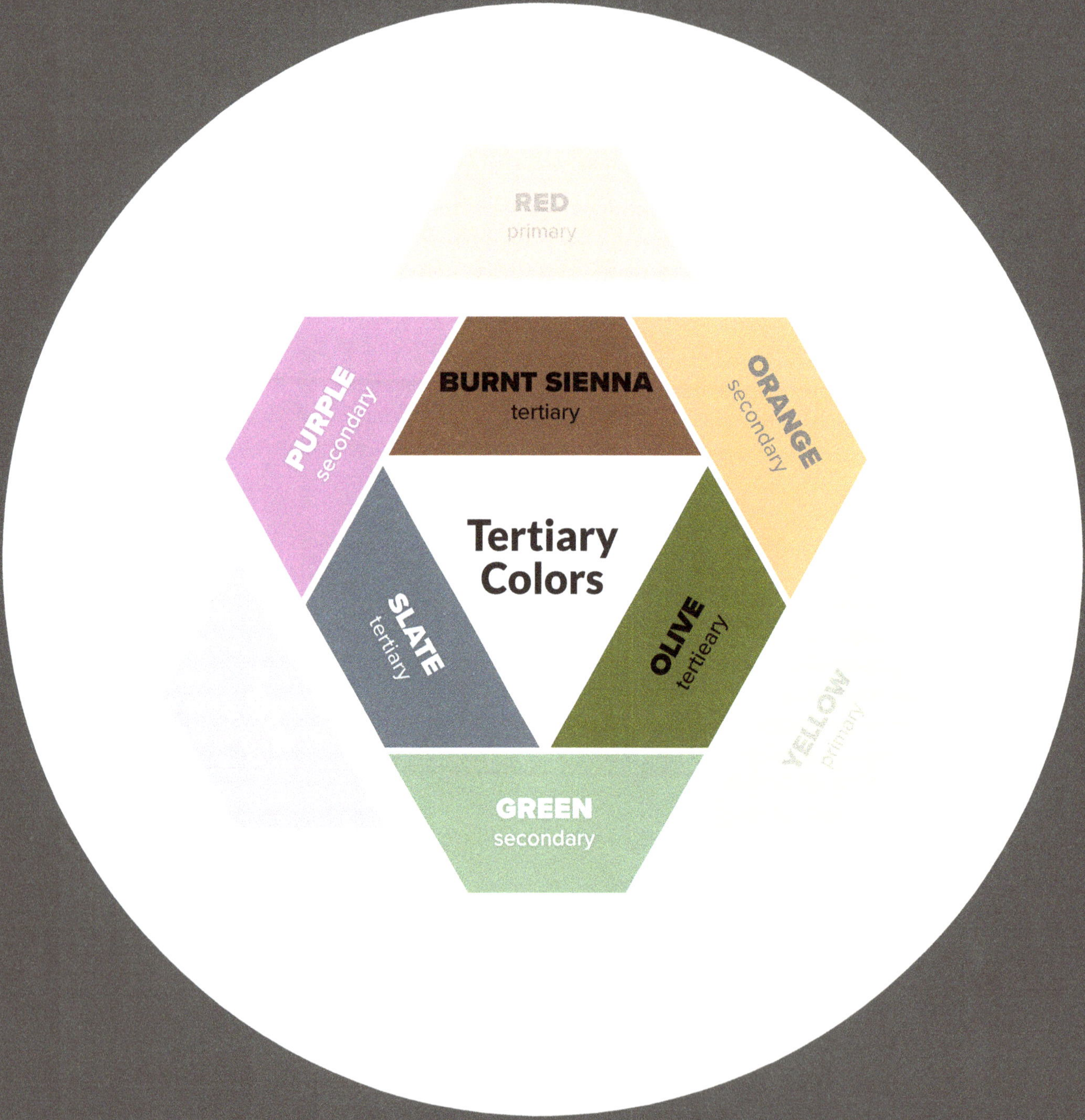

RED
primary

PURPLE
secondary

BURNT SIENNA
tertiary

ORANGE
secondary

Tertiary
Colors

SLATE
tertiary

OLIVE
tertieary

YELLOW
primary

GREEN
secondary

The Grandkids
Tertiary Colors (Born from Secondaries)

If you looked up tertiary colors online, you would believe they are the same as intermediate colors. And you'd be correct, for the most part. One meaning of tertiary is third in importance, which intermediate colors are. But, another definition describes tertiary colors as the result of two secondary colors mixed together, which is my chosen definition. One reason is that it supports my family analogy.

You could say that primary colors are tertiaries' grandparents. They give us some fantastic colors like Sienna (Orange and Purple), Olive (Orange and Green), and Slate (Green and Purple).

Although these colors are not typically found on the basic Newton color wheel, they are still worth considering. These rich, vibrant colors are beautiful and full of potential. Some brands choose to use tertiary colors in their branding. For instance, Burnt Sienna is a popular color choice for many chocolate brands such as Hershey's, Nestle, and Wonka. Olive is another popular color for many olive oil brands, like Olive Grove and L'Olivo. Slate is the main color for Honolulu Beerworks, while Paramount uses a version of Slate in their color palette. Tertiary colors are also quite popular in the world of interior design.

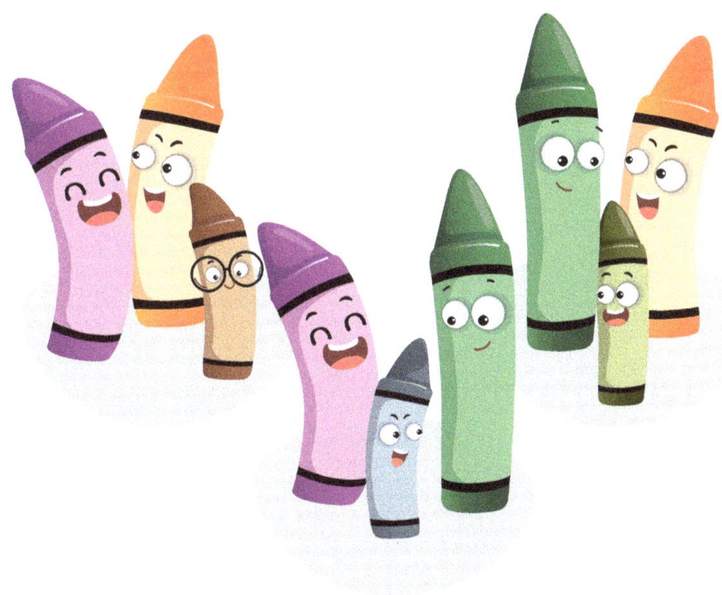

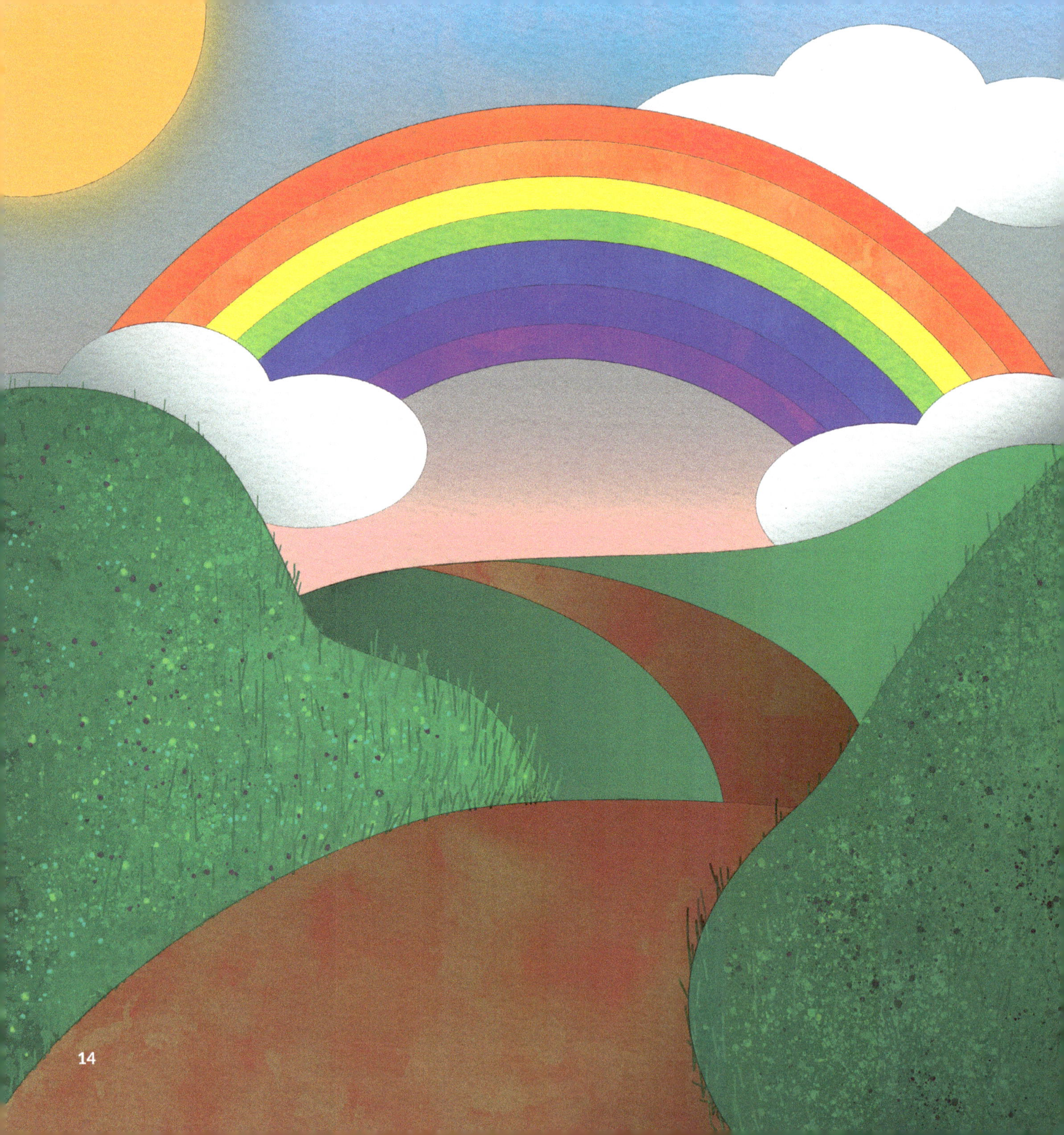

Why Does the Rainbow Have Seven Colors?

Back to Roy G. Biv for a minute… So, you might be asking, "Where is indigo on the color wheel? And why is Violet (an intermediate color) used when all the other colors are primary and secondary?" Well, those are good questions.

There are several ways to answer these. But in my understanding, Violet refers to Purple on my color wheel, and indigo is actually the intermediate color, Violet. You see, the names on the color wheel vary from one interpretation to another. The answer to why indigo is even used as a color of the rainbow by Sir Isaac Newton is, well, political in a way.

In a nutshell, Newton wanted seven colors in the rainbow because seven is the magical number according to ancient Greek philosophy. And why indigo? As it turns out, indigo was a hot commodity at the time.

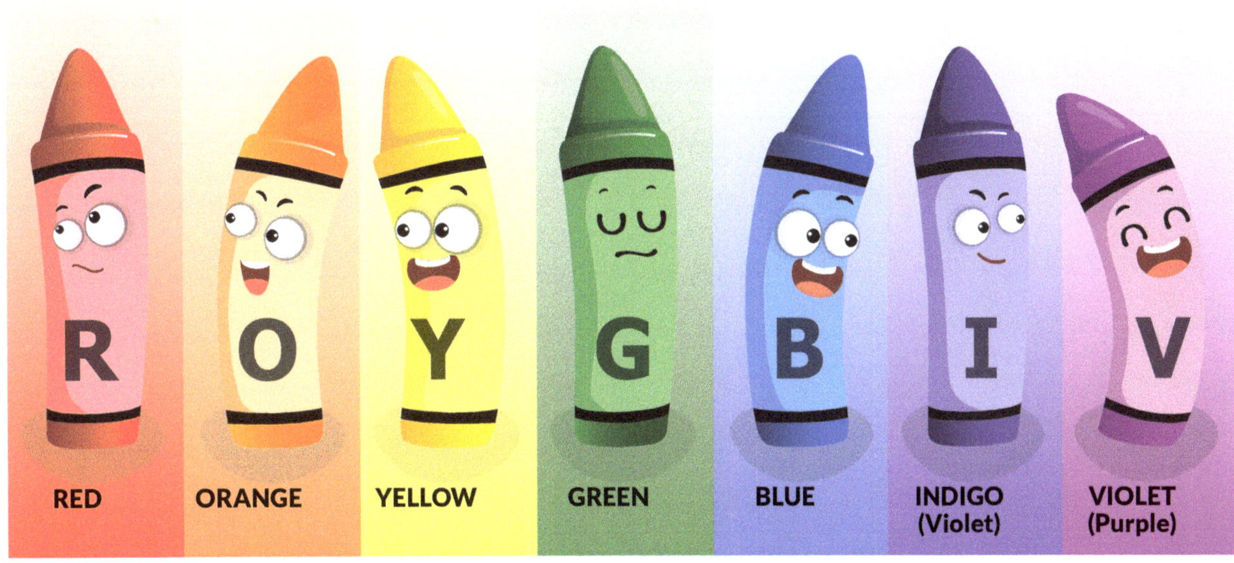

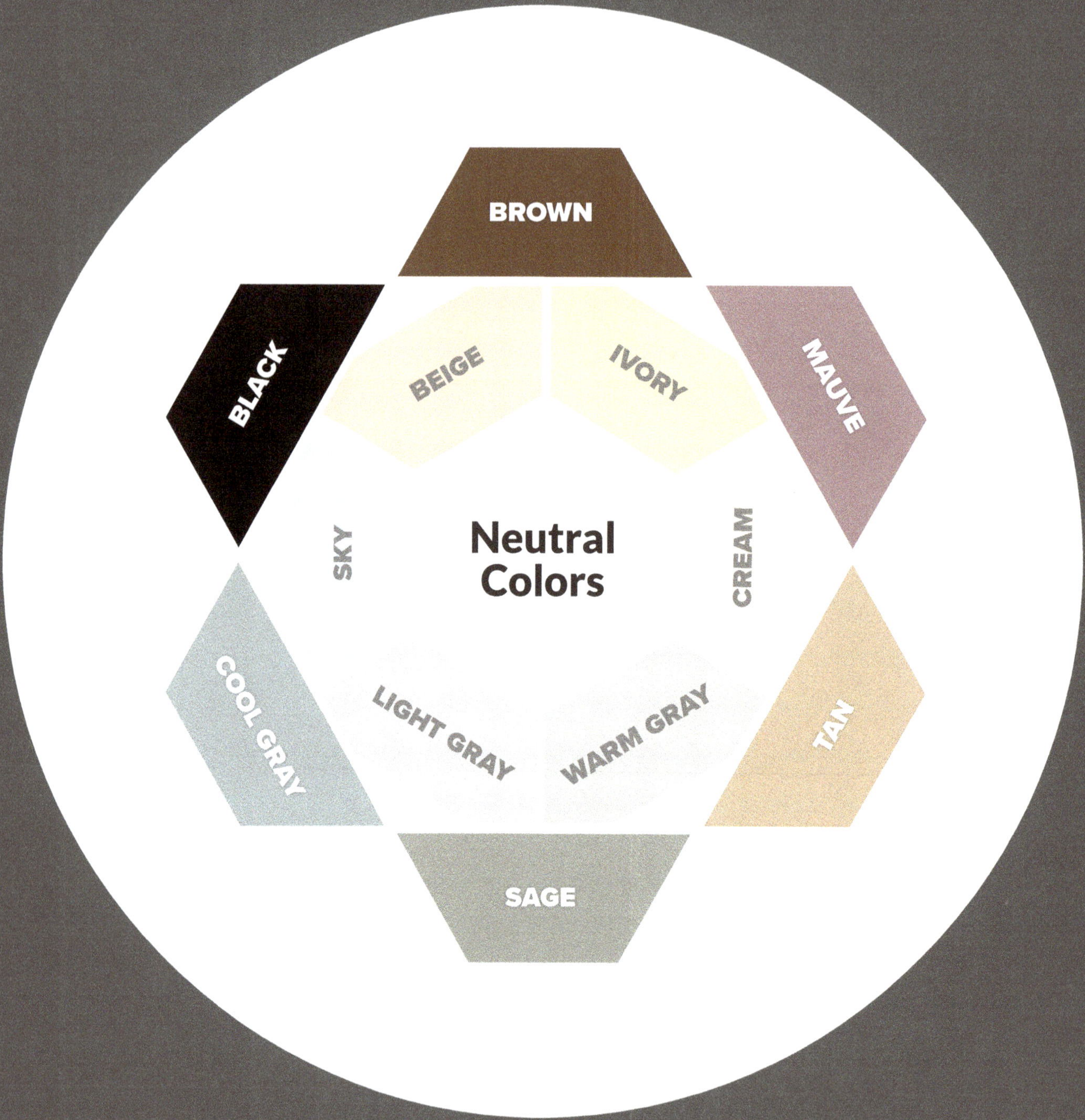

BROWN
BLACK
BEIGE
IVORY
MAUVE
SKY
Neutral Colors
CREAM
COOL GRAY
LIGHT GRAY
WARM GRAY
TAN
SAGE

The Middle Children
Neutrals (Staying out of the Drama)

Neutral colors are, as you guessed, earth tones like Brown, Tan, and Beige. Tertiary colors can fall into this spectrum as well. But did you know that Black, White, and Gray are also considered neutral? Neutral colors are a great way to create contrast or add depth to any visual.

Neutrals are often considered to lack color but typically contain some hue. Beige, cream, and ivory are the colors that first come to mind. Neutral colors are soft and calming. They work well as a background for more vibrant colors.

Neutrals are the most versatile and easy-to-use of all colors. The reason is that our brains tend not to register neutral hues as colors. Have you ever tried to match a White? If you go to a paint store, there are hundreds of White paint colors to choose from. However, because neutrals are so subtle, you can pair them with almost any other color.

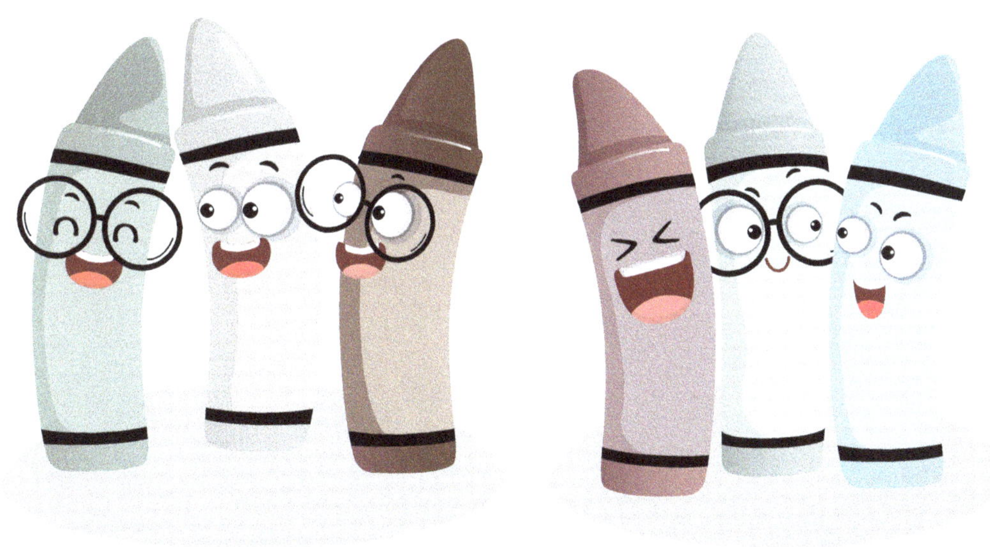

HUE: Pure Color (Hue)
TINT: Hue + White
SHADE: Hue + Black
TONE: Hue + Black + White

Hues, Shades, Tints, & Tones, Oh My!

RED
primary

red-orange
VERMILION
intermediate

ORANGE
secondary

yellow-orange
AMBER
intermediate

YELLOW
primary

yellow-green
CHARTREUSE
intermediate

GREEN
secondary

blue-green
TEAL
intermediate

BLUE
primary

blue-purple
VIOLET
intermediate

PURPLE
secondary

red-purple
MAGENTA
intermediate

Hues, Shades, Tints, and Tones, Oh My!

Three important things to remember about color are the hue (the original color), the value (how light or dark it is), and the saturation (how bright or dull it is).

The **hue** tells us about the position of the specific color in the wheel. In the picture to the left, you can see each hue on the color wheel, along with some shades, tints, and tones.

The hue is the purest form of a color. If you want to change the **value**, there are various ways to do that. You can add a **shade**. Just mix any hue (color) with multiple amounts of Black. A **tint** is created by adding some White.

If you want a **tone** change, mix it with Gray (Black and White). The saturation of the color indicates its brightness. The brighter the color, the more **saturated** it is. The less hue that it has, the more **desaturated** it is.

By the way, the color you start with doesn't necessarily have to be a primary, secondary, intermediate, or tertiary. It can be any color that you've created.

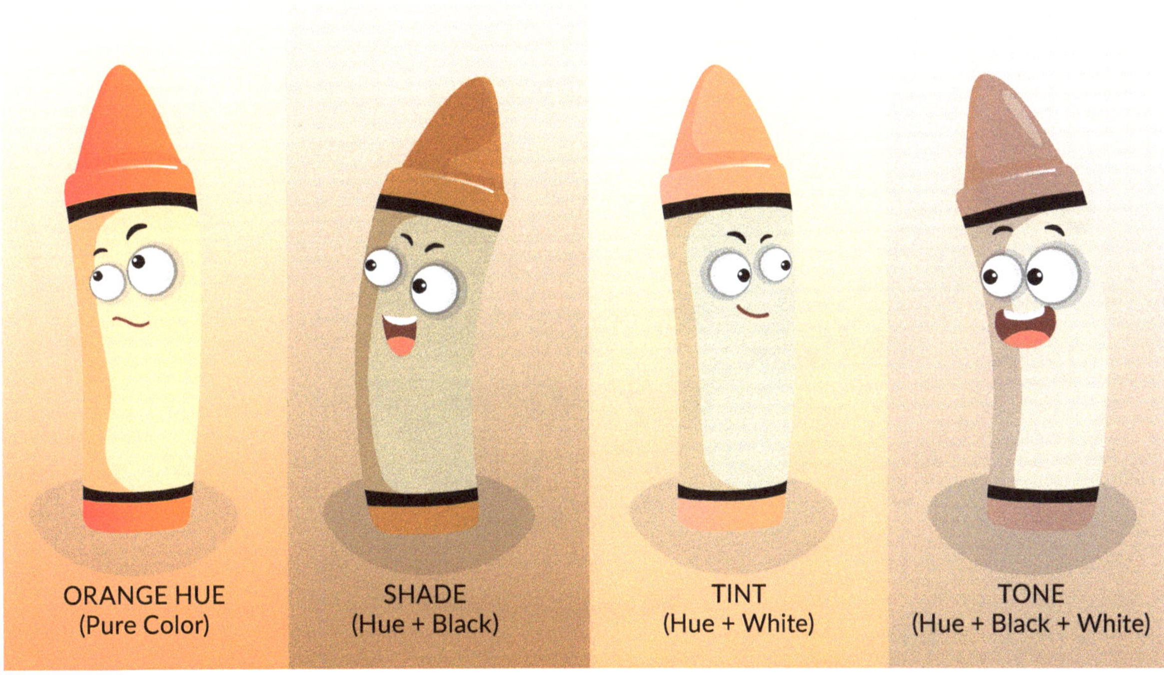

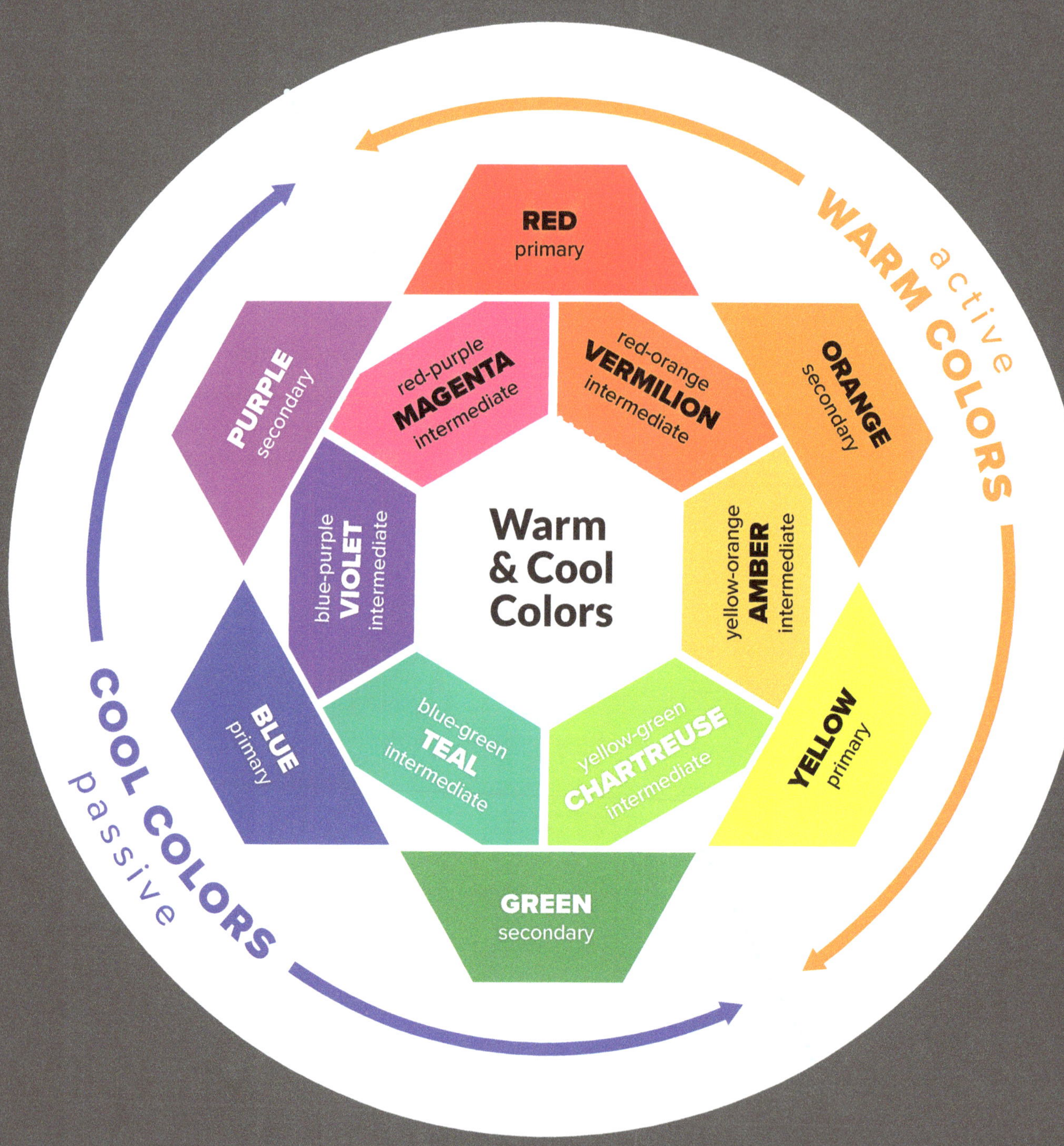

active
WARM COLORS
COOL COLORS
passive
RED
primary
red-purple
MAGENTA
intermediate
red-orange
VERMILION
intermediate
ORANGE
secondary
PURPLE
secondary
blue-purple
VIOLET
intermediate
Warm
& Cool
Colors
yellow-orange
AMBER
intermediate
BLUE
primary
blue-green
TEAL
intermediate
yellow-green
CHARTREUSE
intermediate
YELLOW
primary
GREEN
secondary

If Colors Took a Personality Test

Can colors have a personality? Well, of course, they can! They can be brilliant, dull, shiny, blah, etc. But they can also be active or passive. If you draw a line through the middle of the color wheel between Yellow and Chartreuse on one side and Purple and Magenta on the other, you will get two separate color palettes. The **active warm colors** (Reds, Oranges, and Yellows) and the **passive cool colors** (Greens, Blues, and Purples).

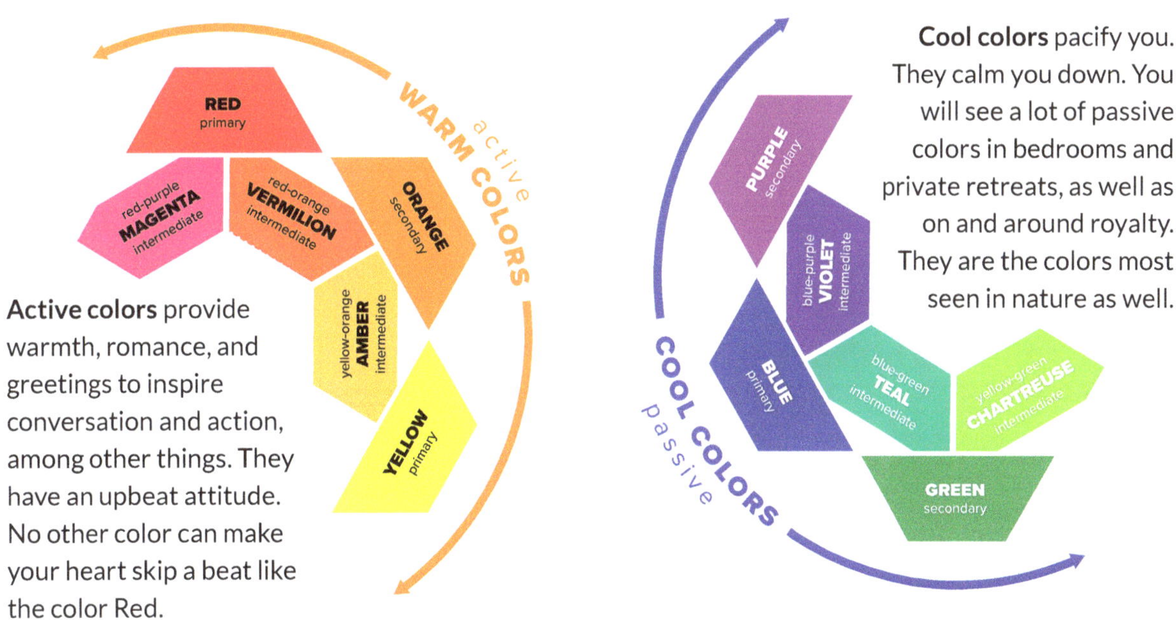

Active colors provide warmth, romance, and greetings to inspire conversation and action, among other things. They have an upbeat attitude. No other color can make your heart skip a beat like the color Red.

Cool colors pacify you. They calm you down. You will see a lot of passive colors in bedrooms and private retreats, as well as on and around royalty. They are the colors most seen in nature as well.

So, now that we have a grasp on the color wheel let's look at what it can do for us. Colors impact the message you want to send, and knowing which color to use can significantly enhance the effectiveness of your message or vice versa. In the next chapter, we'll look at how to choose colors that go together.

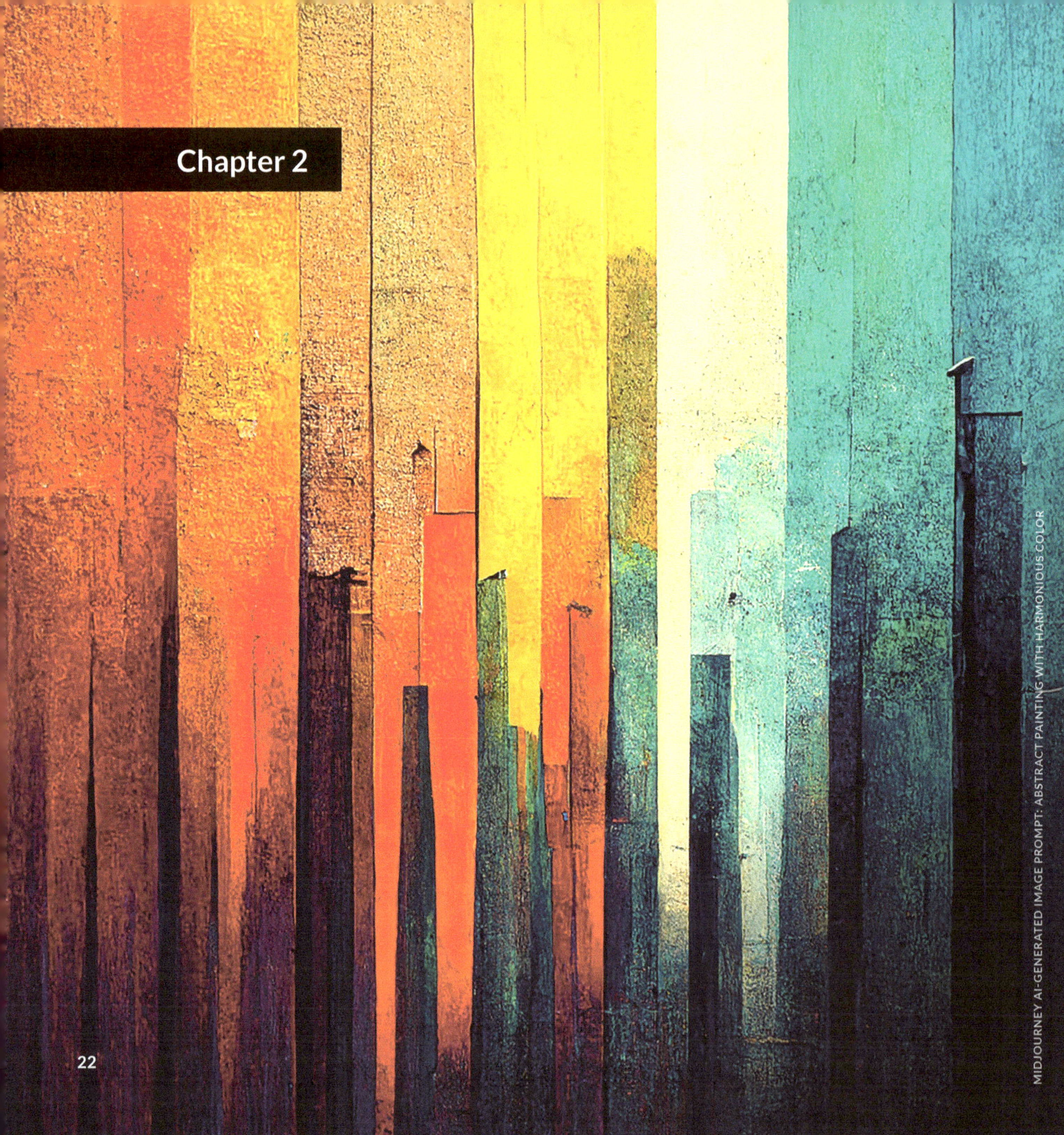
Chapter 2
22
MIDJOURNEY AI-GENERATED IMAGE PROMPT: ABSTRACT PAINTING WITH HARMONIOUS COLOR

Perfect Harmony

Where does our colorful family go next? Whether designing a logo, creating a website, or choosing what to wear, we all make decisions about color combinations throughout our day. Some people (graphic designers, like me) do it a lot. In fact, my work heavily depends on it.

Whatever you use color combinations on, you want it to be something that will not only make you look good, but in business, you also want to entice people to buy your brand or service. A winning combination could mean an eye-catching visual. It could make your message come to life. It can set the viewer's mood and influence their emotions and perceptions.

What it all comes down to is color theory. It would take days if I sat down to explain it to you in detail. There are volumes on color theory to be found at the library or bookstore by numerous authors that go into great detail. When I was researching for this book, it was easy for me to go down a deep rabbit hole. But that's because it's all pretty fascinating to me. I had to focus on simplifying it for you, and I hope I've done that. Understanding the color wheel is the first step. Now, let's harmonize.

What is Color Harmony?

Color harmony is precisely as the name suggests. When you think of harmony, you think of music, poetry, color, or anything else arranged in a way that sounds or looks pleasing.

Color harmony is visual color elements arranged pleasingly. It can engage a user and communicate with them on a subliminal level. If the colors are harmonious, the result is smooth and exciting. If not, the result can be chaos and boring. You cannot wait to get that thing out of your head.

Find the Perfect Relationship

It helps to work with a set number of colors when designing. Whether working on an art project, interior design, infographic, wardrobe, or anything in between, your color scheme/combination could have as few as two colors to more than 20 (although I would not recommend that). By combining two or more colors, you can create multiple palettes.

Let's follow our Crayon family as they navigate relationships. These are typical color schemes that can be a starting point for you. They are not steadfast rules. Instead, look at them as guidelines—a jump start for your own color palette.

Monochromatic Color Scheme
TINTS, TONES AND SHADES OF A COLOR (HUE)

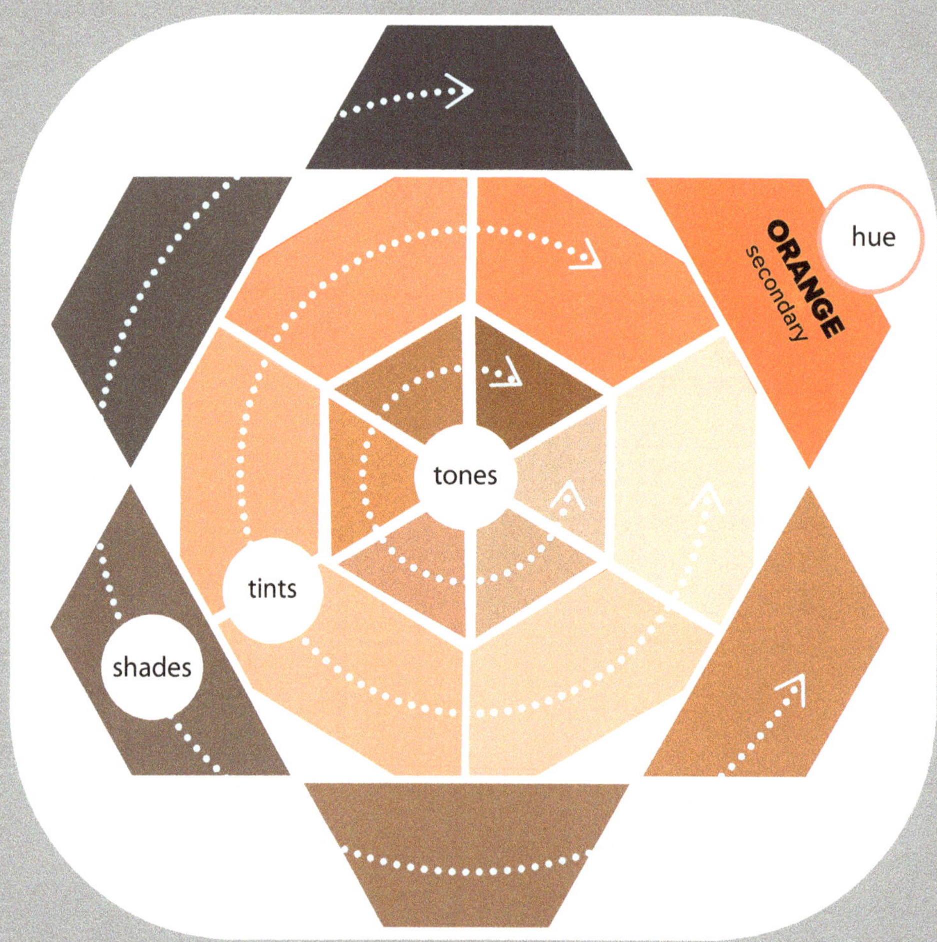

IN THIS EXAMPLE:

The pure color (hue) is used as the base color. Then
various tones (+gray), tints (+white), and shades (+black)
make up the rest of the monochromatic color scheme.

Obsession
Monochromatic Color Scheme

Yup. There are monochromatic (one-color) color schemes out there. They utilize variations of a single color (hue) to send the message. You can create an entire palette by combining White, Gray, and Black with a single hue. Those tints, tones, and shades discussed in Chapter 1 provide highlights and shadows to spruce up an otherwise flat color palette.

One of the reasons why this color scheme is so pleasing to the eye is its versatility. Using a single hue without the gradations runs the risk of being too dull. However, using different tones, shades, and tints of the same color in the same visual is easy on the eyes, and there's no clash. When you use a monochromatic scheme, it won't fall flat while keeping the overall color combination minimal.

Those in favor of minimalism love this scheme. That's why monochromatic schemes are so popular these days. You can see them on various branding assets. Also, if you want content to stand out, a monochromatic theme is the perfect choice for the background.

Remember that it doesn't mean you must go with a dull color. For example, Orange is far from boring. It means that the scheme

you select should work well with the context of the visual you are designing. Sometimes, monochromatic schemes pair perfectly with other schemes. That's right, you can add to and combine schemes to suit your purpose.

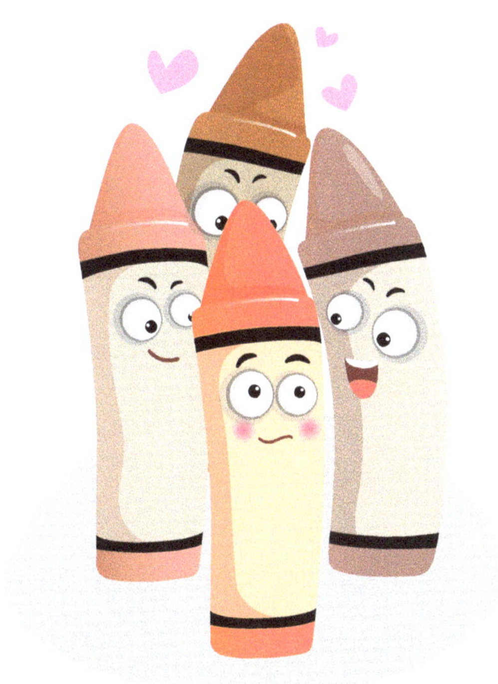

Complementary Color Scheme
OPPOSITES

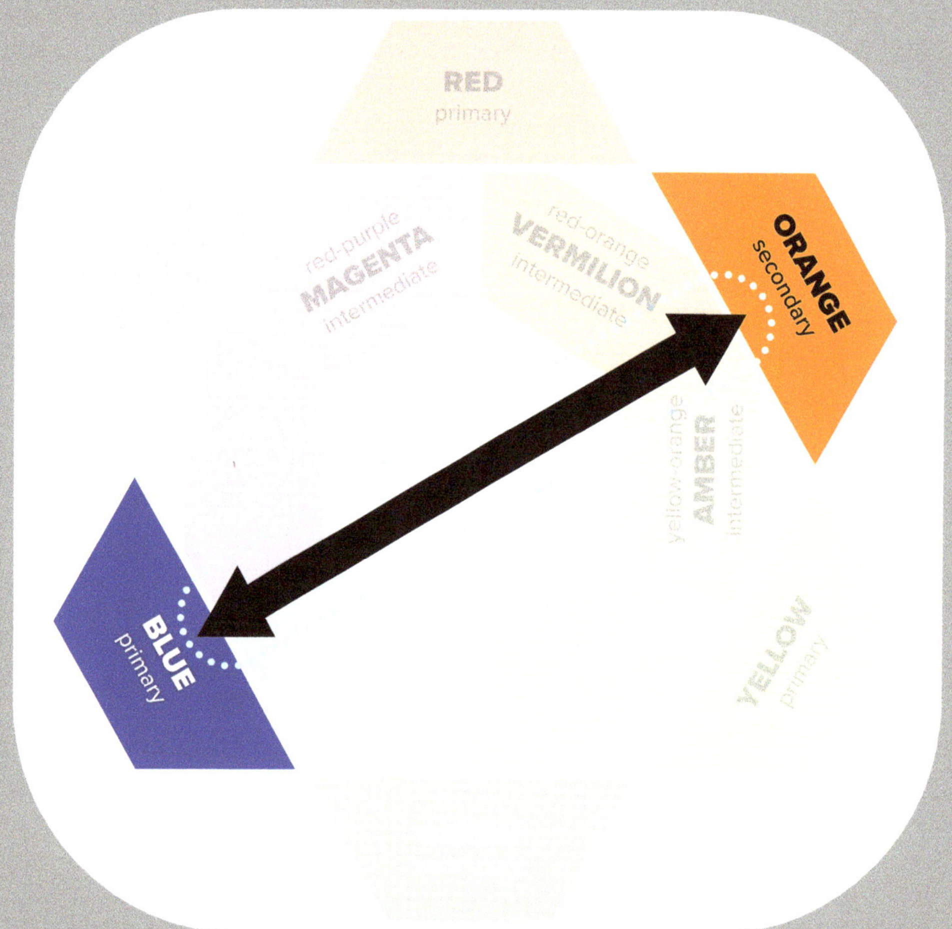

IN THIS EXAMPLE:

Blue, a primary color, is complementary to Orange, a
secondary color. Also, note that intermediate colors
always complement intermediate colors.

Opposites Attract
Complementary Color Scheme

This color scheme exists on both sides of the color wheel. It's created by selecting a color on one side of the wheel and the color directly opposite on the other side, one cool color and one warm color.

This scheme provides a contrasting theme for all your visuals. It can be a bit intense at full saturation, and that may be what you're going for. If you want to tone it down a little, go with shades, tints, and tones of the complementary hues, just like we do with the monochromatic scheme we just talked about.

You've heard the saying: "opposites attract." Well, that's what makes this scheme so popular. The Christmas combination of Red and Green is an example, as well as popular school colors like Purple and Yellow or Blue and Orange. Also, you can use this scheme to highlight the part of a design you want your

viewers to focus on more. For example, you could use a monochromatic Blue theme and Orange (its complement) as a CTA (call-to-action) button to draw attention. Incorporating a scheme that pairs warm and cool colors always adds visual impact.

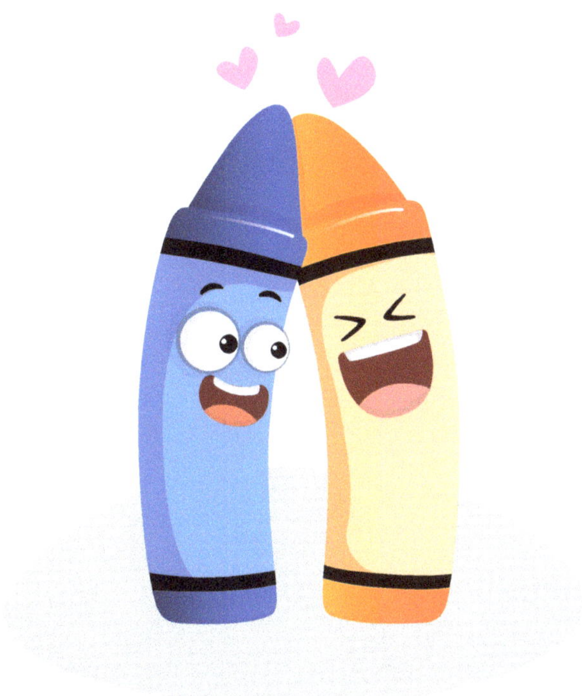

Triadic Color Scheme

FORMS A TRIANGLE

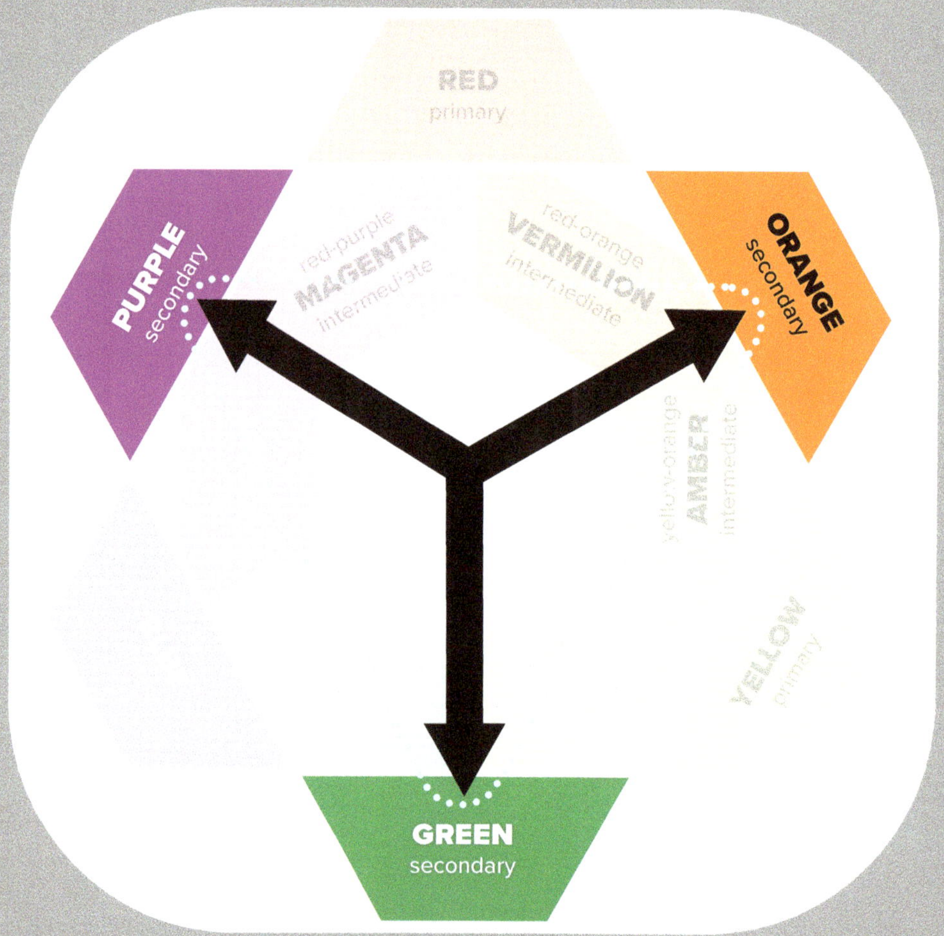

IN THIS EXAMPLE:

The primary colors are considered a triadic color scheme,
as is the secondary colors. A triadic color scheme forms
an equilateral triangle.

Three's Company
Triadic Color Scheme

Pick three colors on the color wheel that are at an equal distance from one another. They should form a perfect triangle.

Thus, the word triadic. As you may have noticed, primary colors (Red, Yellow, and Blue) and secondary colors (Orange, Green, and Purple) are triadic color schemes. You can create two additional triadic color schemes with intermediate colors (Vermilion/Chartreuse/Violet, and Magenta/Amber/Teal).

This color scheme provides more variety as it is truly a colorful palette.

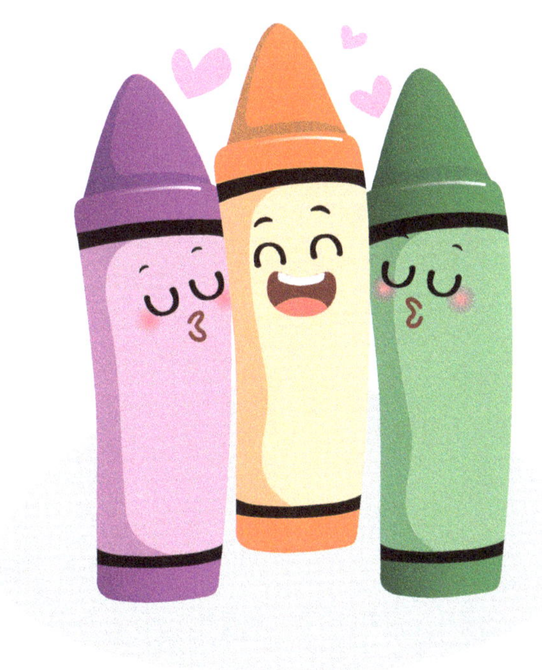

Split Complementary Color Scheme
NEIGHBORS OF COMPLEMENTARY COLOR

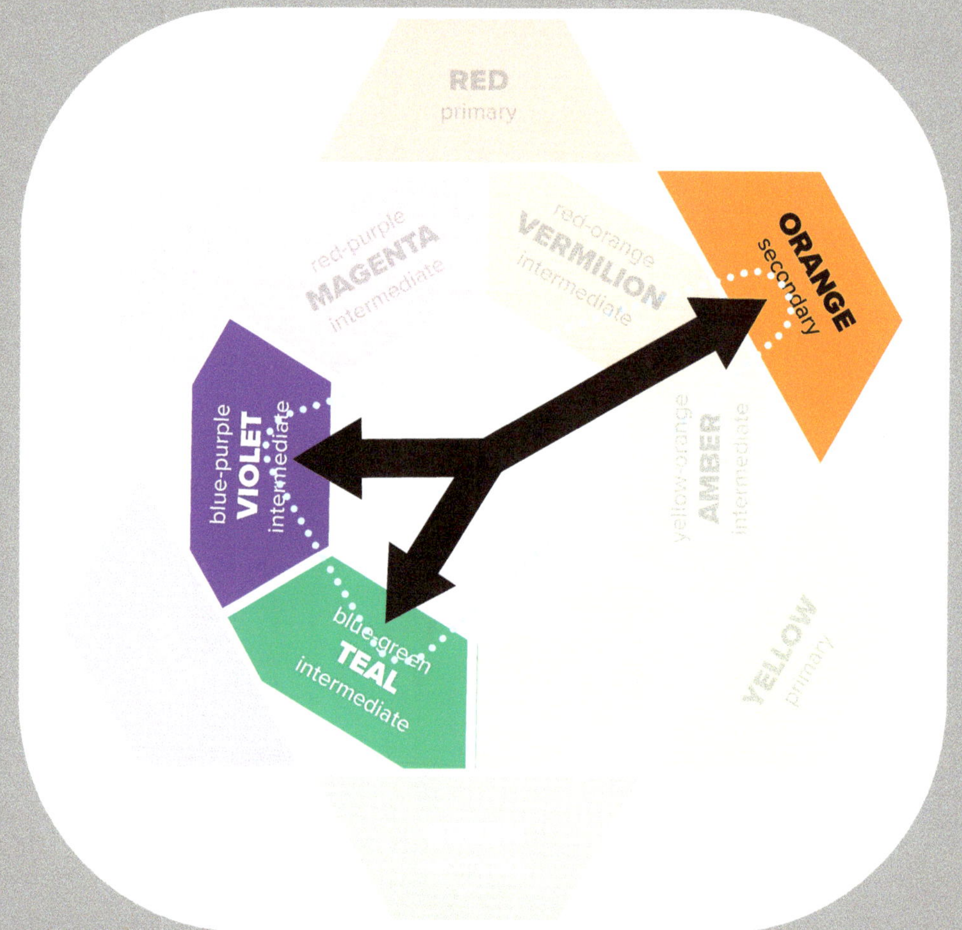

IN THIS EXAMPLE:

Blue is complementary to Orange, both secondary colors. So, in a split-complementary color scheme, Teal and Violet, intermediate colors, are used because they are the direct neighbors of Blue. This scheme forms a triangle, but unlike the Triadic scheme it is not equilateral.

The Third Wheel
Split-Complementary Color Scheme

This color scheme is similar to the complementary color scheme with just one difference. Instead of using two colors that are opposite of each other, it uses three colors. Pick a color on one side of the wheel and then choose the direct neighbors of the contrasting color on the opposite side to form a skinny triangle, unlike the triadic color scheme that uses an equilateral triangle. One warm color and two cool colors, or one cool color and two warm colors, will make up this color scheme.

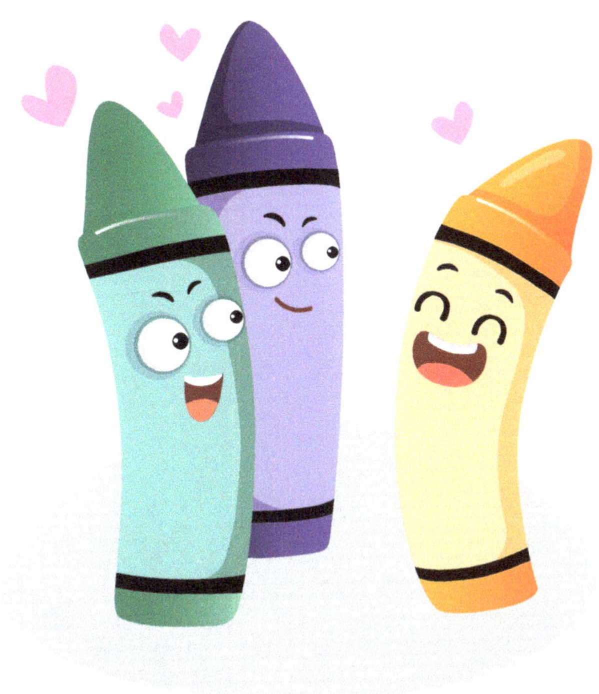

Analagous Color Scheme

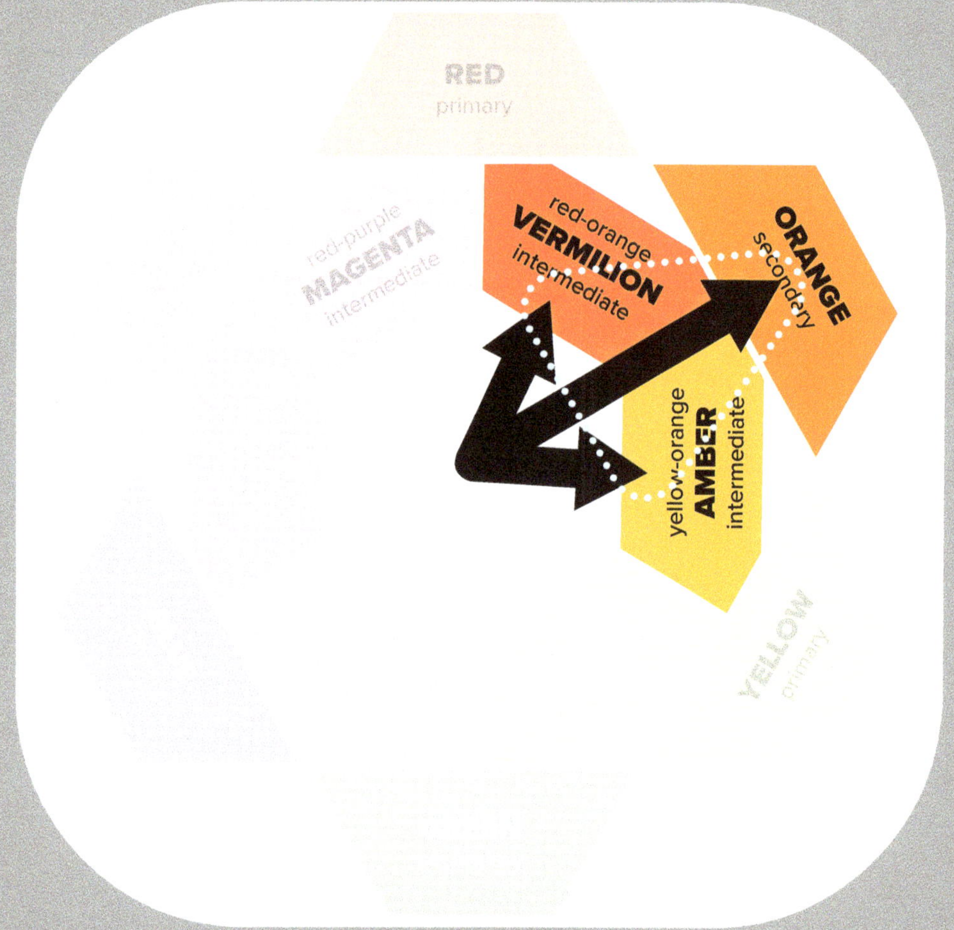

IN THIS EXAMPLE:

The center color of this three-color scheme is Orange, a secondary color, and its two neighbors, Vermillion and Amber, both intermediates. Unlike Triadic and Split-Complementary schemes, this one only uses one side of the color wheel. However, there can be one warm and two cool colors or vice versa in this scheme.

Birds of a Feather
Analogous Color Scheme

The analogous color scheme is the opposite of the complementary color scheme. Instead of choosing two colors on opposite sides of the wheel, you choose three colors that border each other on the wheel. It can look similar to a monochromatic scheme. You first select a base color and then the two neighboring colors.

It's evident in the name. The word "analogous" means something that is closely related. This color scheme is an easy one to work with, so if you ever find yourself confused and not knowing which color scheme to pick up, go with an analogous scheme.

They say, "birds of a feather flock together." Well, that's so true with this color scheme. Just look to nature. You will find a lot of birds, as well as oceans and other elements, that incorporate the analogous color scheme. All these things immediately instill in you a sense of calm and peace.

Try adding some oomph to this scheme using colors on the border between warm and cool. Imagine Amber, Yellow, and Chartreuse.

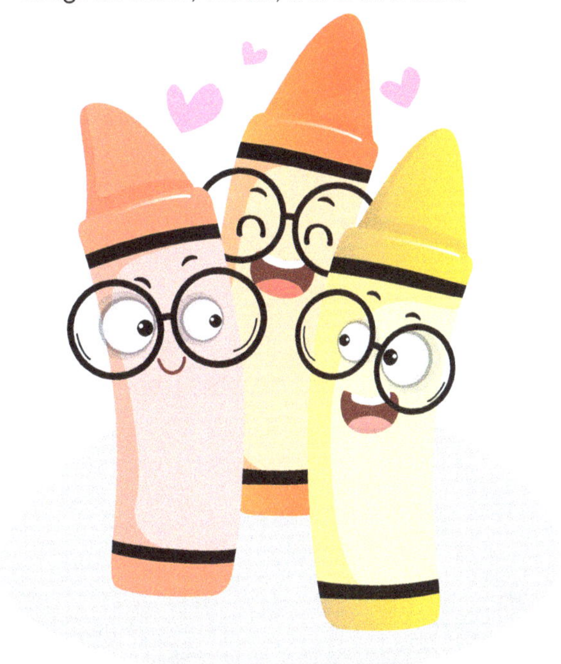

Tetradic Color Scheme
TWO COMPLEMENTARY SCHEMES

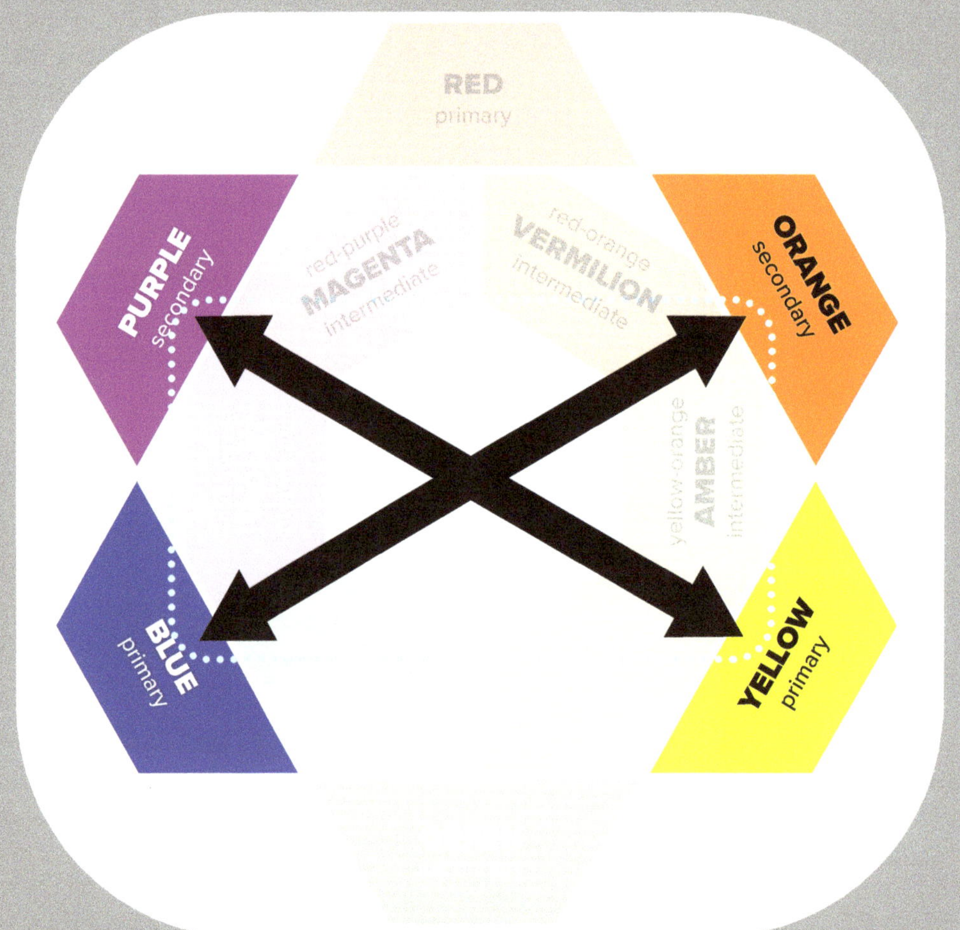

IN THIS EXAMPLE:

Purple complements Yellow and Orange complements Blue and together they form a rectangle.
Remember: primaries always complement secondaries, and vice versa. Plus, intermediates always complement intermediates. Thus, this color scheme could produce a trapezoid shape instead of a rectangle on this color wheel.

Double Dating
Tetradic Color Scheme

This color scheme uses four colors—two complimentary schemes combined. It's certainly fun when two pairs of complimentary colors get together. But, as I said before, these schemes are just a starting point. You can add to or combine schemes to achieve your purpose. The tetradic color scheme gives you two colors from each side of the color wheel, allowing versatility and bringing different personalities into your branding.

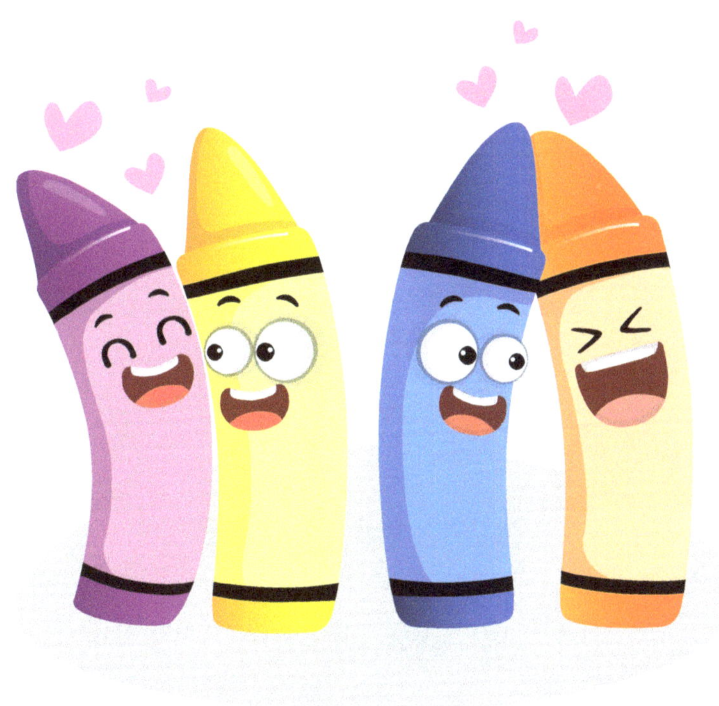

Achromatic Color Scheme
VOID OF COLOR

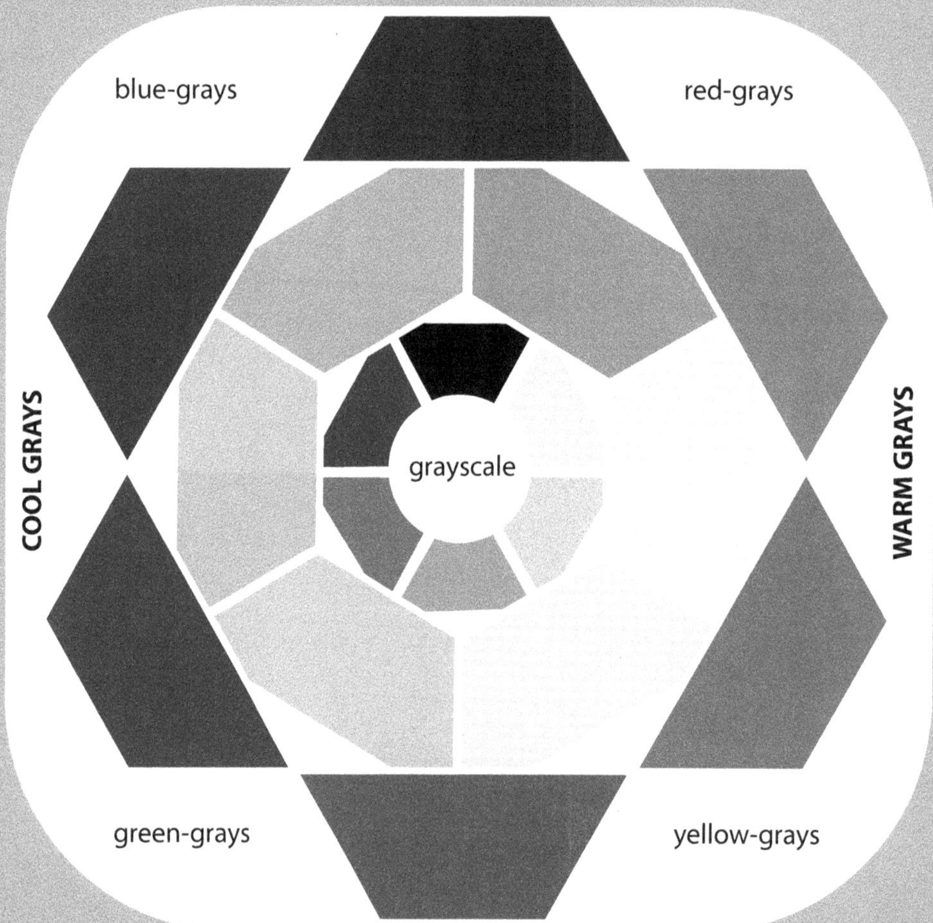

IN THIS EXAMPLE:

Although this scheme is essentially colors that are void of color (grayscale), it is acceptable to add a slight amount of color to the scheme to add a richness to it.

Noir

Achromatic Color Scheme

This scheme has recently seen a considerable rise in popularity, no matter what design field we look at. Like Film Noir, it can be dark and gloomy, consisting of monochromatic colors like White, Black, and Gray. However, it can include neutral colors like Brown, Tan, or similar hues. One important thing to mention here is the addition of tone, tint, and shade to ensure that the colors are all desaturated, meaning all or most of the color is stripped from the hue.

Even though the word achromatic means "void of hue," it's okay to have minimal color. You can have a Cool-Gray palette that consists of Green-Gray and Blue-Gray colors or a Warm-Gray palette with Yellow-Gray and Red-Gray colors.

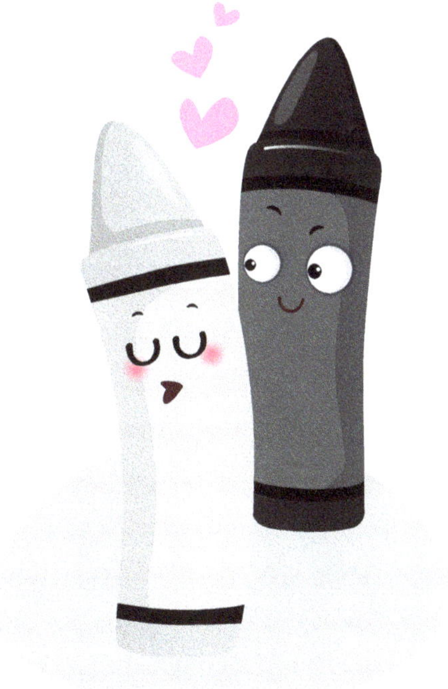

Now that you know all about colors, their importance, their overall schemes, and more, you must be itching to know what this all means. Well, let's find out in the next chapter.

Summing it Up

In Chapter 1, we explored the origins of color theory. Then we were introduced to the colorful Crayon family who took us for a ride on the color wheel. And finally, we found out that colors do indeed have personalities. In Chapter 2, we peeked in on the "dating" relationships of the Crayons as we explored color schemes that bring harmony to our color palettes. Why are these things important to know, you ask? It helps us, as entrepreneurs, tell our story. Colors and how they interact is part of that story. So, if you want to know how much you've retained in Part 1, take the test below.

What Have You Learned So Far?

Let's test your knowledge about the color wheel and color harmonies. Answer the questions below, then compare them to the answer key on page 114 to find out how you did.

1. What are the three primary colors (hint: the parents)? _______________________________

____

2. Who invented the color wheel (and discovered the rainbow)? _______________________

3. Who (or what) is ROY G. BIV? _____________

____

____

____

4. What are secondary colors (or children) born from?_______________________________

____

5. Hue is another way of saying color. True or False? _______________________________

6. What two "personalities" of color divide the color wheel in half? _______________________

____

7. Tertiary colors can be another way of saying intermediate colors. In this book tertiary colors are made from two secondary colors. True or False? _______________

8. What can be added to a color to make it a shade of the hue? _______________________

9. What are the three types of colors on the color wheel? (hint: parents, children, and

grandchildren) ________________________

____

____

10. How are intermediate colors made? ______

____

____

11. If I add White to a color, I'm making a

______________ of that color.

12. A color scheme void of color, or desaturated using shades, tint, and tones, is called

________________________________ .

13. What color scheme is used in this image?

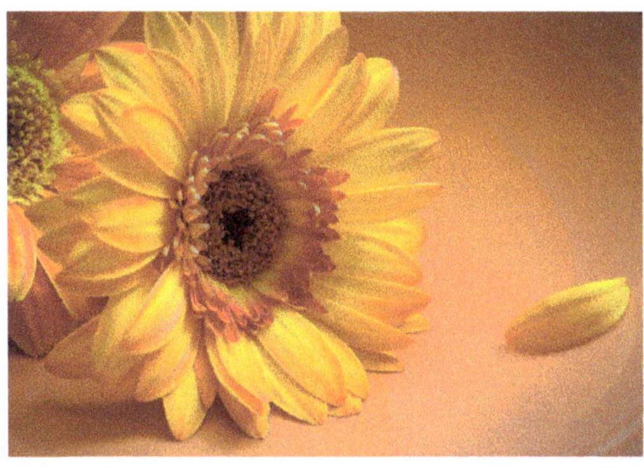

____

14. What color scheme is used in this image?

____

15. If I was obsessed with a color and wanted
to build my color palette with shades, tints
and tones of that color, what scheme would
I use? ____________________________

16. Which color scheme forms an equilateral
triangle on the color wheel? ____________

____

17. The Achromatic color scheme consists of
three colors that are side-by-side on the
color wheel. True or False? ____________

18. A color scheme made up of two complementary pairs of colors is called __________

____

19. A spit complementary scheme consists of
two colors on one side of the color wheel
and one color on the other side of the color
wheel. True or False? ____________________

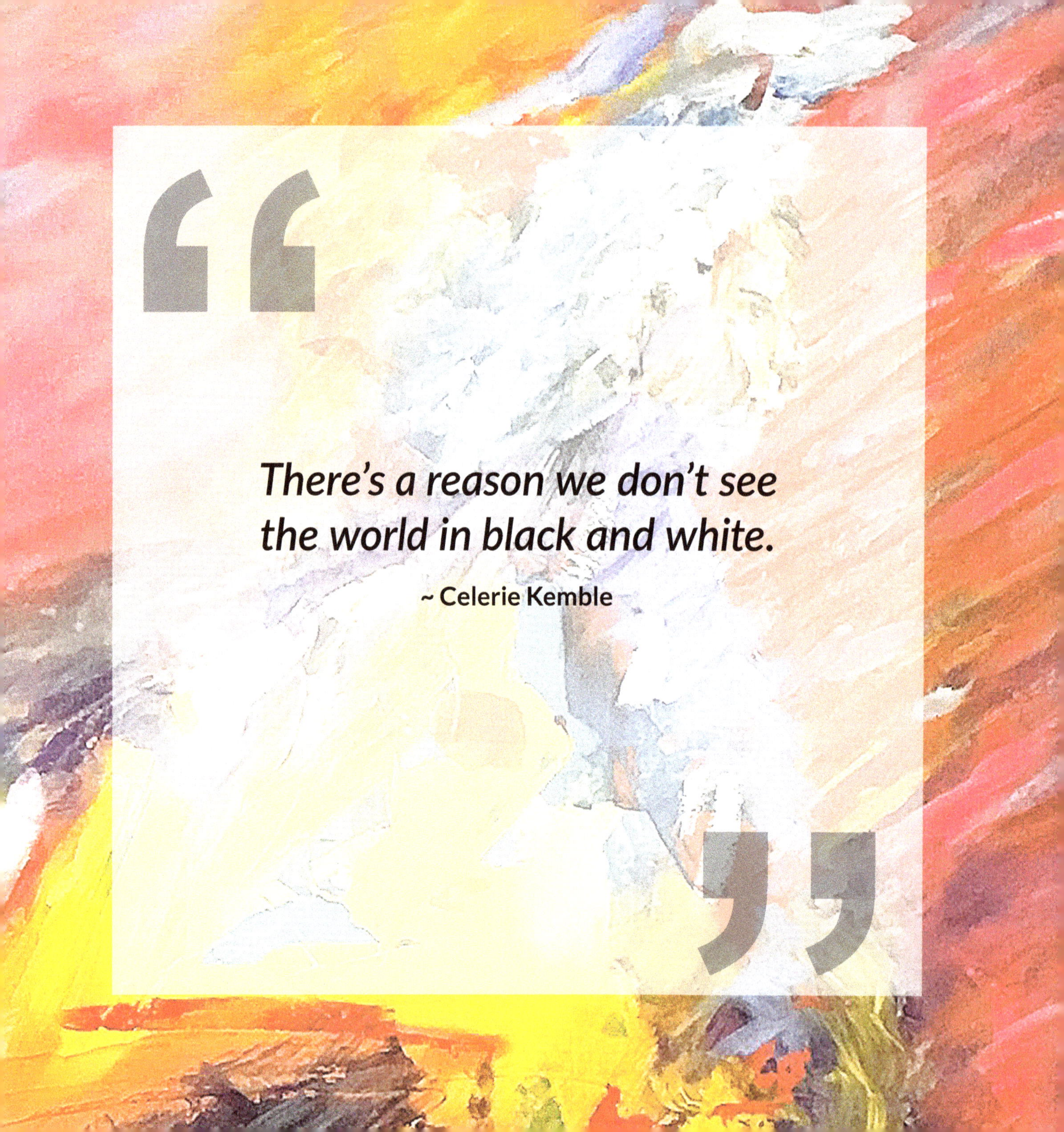
There's a reason we don't see
the world in black and white.
~ Celerie Kemble

PART 2: UNDERSTANDING HOW WE SEE COLOR

[COLOR SYSTEMS]

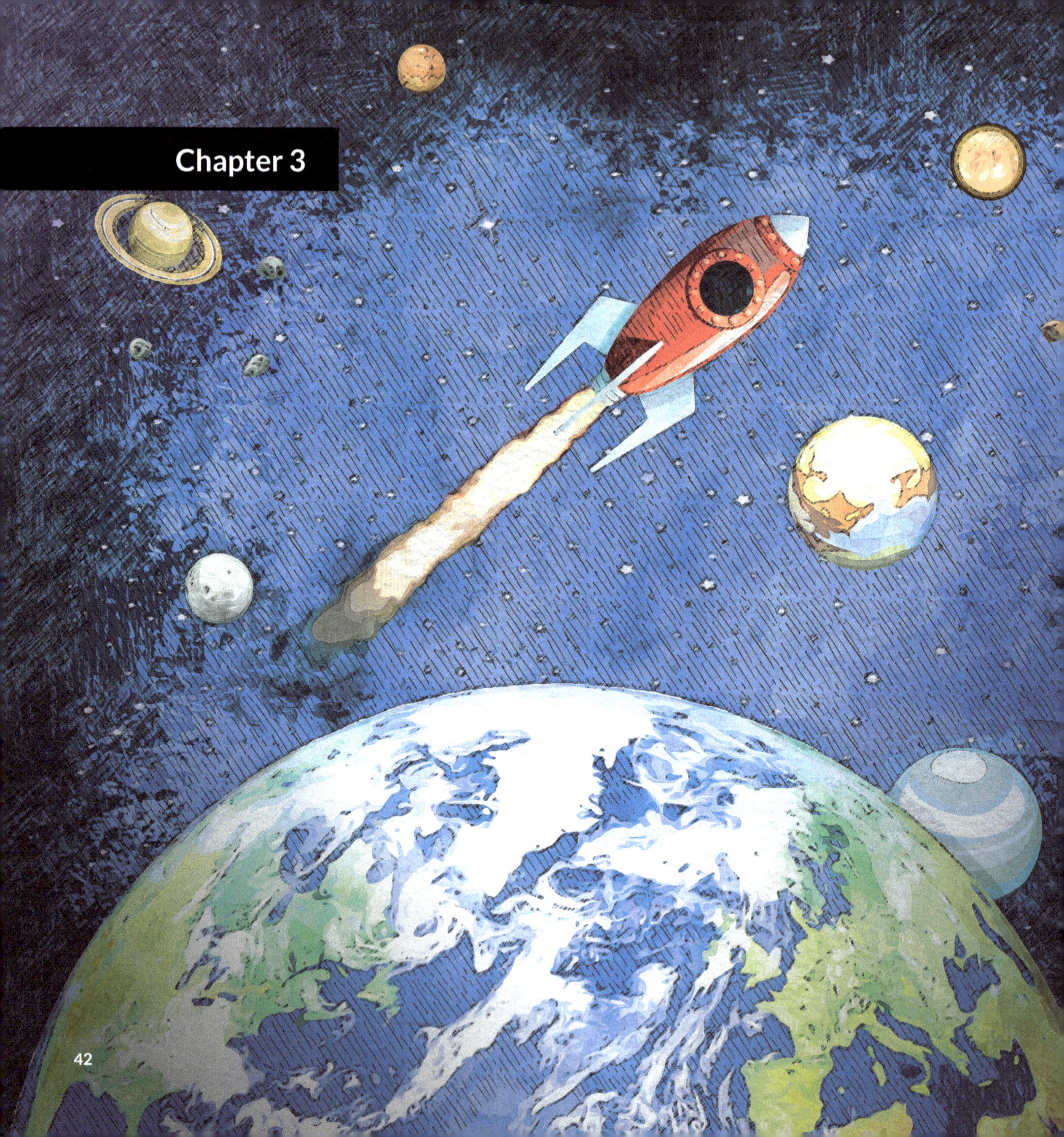
Chapter 3

Space and Systems That Color Our World

So, now that we know the basics of color, you're probably wondering why it's important? Well, for one thing, as an entrepreneur, ads, websites, social media posts, and printed collateral are an everyday part of your business. The better you know your colors, the more you can make your branding stand out with attractive communications and—more importantly—make it engaging.

That is why this topic is helpful for business owners and crucial for us graphic designers, web designers, social media managers, and anyone who has anything to do with business and its communications with their target audience.

Let me ask you a question. When your graphic designer or web designer talks to you about using RGB or CMYK, do you understand what that means? Or do you feel like you are in outer space?

If you're like many people in the business world, you may have a basic or vague idea about these terms at best. To others, it's like an alien language. Some clients look at me with a spaced-out expression when I start talking to them about CMYK or RGB, like I'm talking in a foreign language.

Let's face it. Unless you work with color every day, chances are you have never encountered some of these terms. And now that you're in business, you come up against them every time you turn around. Colors are everywhere, but it's only a subject you think about if you're in business for yourself or you're a graphic designer.

That's why I wanted to give you the low down on it so you can be an informed part of the conversation the next time you sit with your designer, publisher, or web developer.

Color Systems vs. Color Space

Before we get into the whole color systems discussion, I want to ask you one thing.

What color do you think of when you think of Coca-Cola? Red, right? And not just any Red.

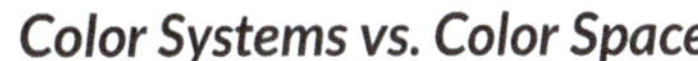

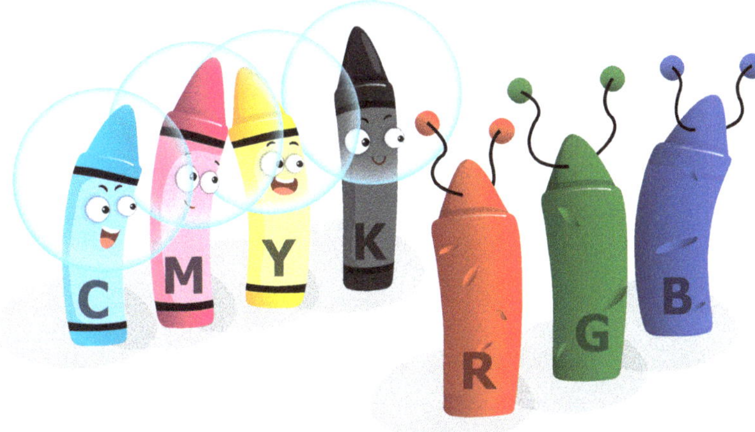

COLOR: How We See It

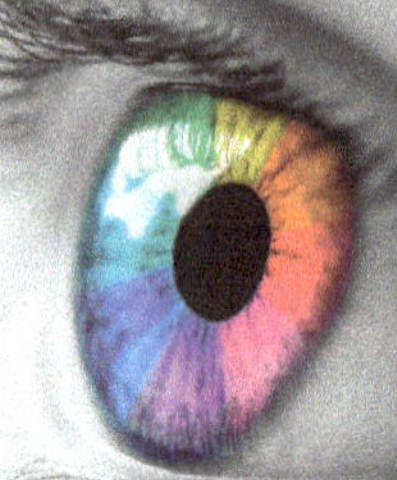

Coca-Cola Red. We'll discuss what could've led Coca-Cola to choose Red in Part 3, *How Color Makes Us Feel*. But for now, we'll talk about making that Red color consistent. You'll notice that Coca-Cola's Red always stays consistent across all channels, including TV, social media, magazines, websites, in-store merchandising, billboards, packaging, etc. The company spends a fortune ensuring its brand color is represented equally on all mediums.

You may not know this, but this type of consistency is not easily achieved. Literally hundreds of designers, printers, artists, and more are working on a major brand like this on a global scale. Just think about all the ways their brand is visualized every day. There are computers, laptops, tablets, iPads, mobile screens, banners, signage, magazines, and more.

Now, don't worry. We're professionals. We know how to make this happen. To be frank, not everybody has the budget for something this big. But relax! By the time you finish this book, you'll be able to manage all the variations of your logo and all your visuals. Becoming aware of universal color systems we use daily will help ensure your message is the same across all your advertising channels.

Color systems are based on how light affects the colors we see. The two major color systems are **subtractive** and **additive**, each specific to certain mediums. For instance, print and screen have two separate systems that we call **space**. Specifically, in print (subtractive), it's the **CMYK color space**, and on-screen (additive), it's the **RGB color space**. FYI, these are not the only two color spaces, but they are the most common.

Let's say you want to use your photo, painting, or even a digitally drawn image in either color space. Care must be taken to be sure these works of art look the same no matter where or how they are processed. The same Red could look Blood Red on one **platform** (brochure, social media post, billboard, video, etc.) and Bright Red on another. The lack of consistency reduces the impact of your message.

What complicates matters is that these spaces each have their own primary colors. So, if you're relating them to the color wheel in Part 1, you will find it doesn't quite match. Although color theory remains the same. But, a file meant for one space will look totally wrong when viewed in another. You may have already experienced this. And there's more... Just because your image is the correct color space doesn't mean the color is right. I know it gets confusing. **Color correction** is sometimes needed. Professionals have the tools to make the colors match perfectly to your products or works of art.

My Kind of Math!

I'm using the terms additive and subtractive here to highlight the differences between the two color systems. You typically won't hear professionals referring to them in this way. They usually just call them by their letters: CMYK or RGB.

The **subtractive** (or CMYK) model absorbs or reflects light. The colors you don't see are

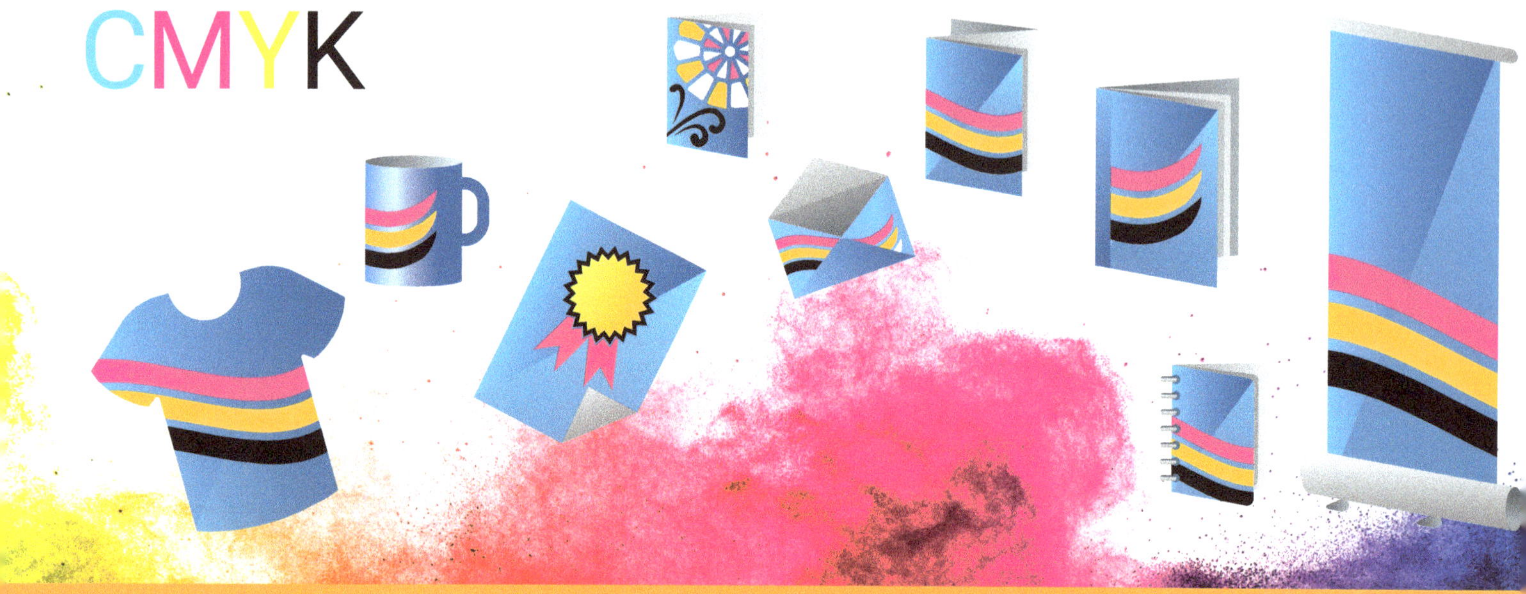

CMYK
IN PRINT 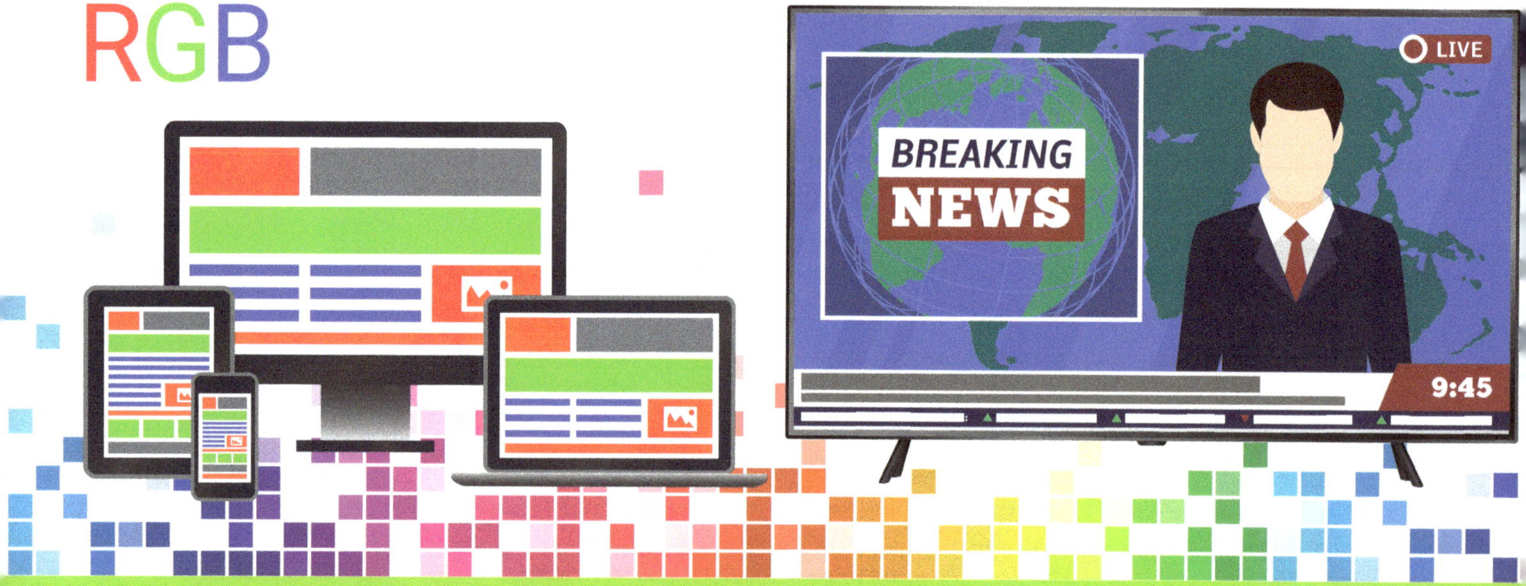
RGB
BREAKING
NEWS
LIVE
9:45
ON SCREEN
46

absorbed (subtracted), and the ones you are supposed to see reflect back to your eyes.

In other words, objects or materials—such as paper, canvas, plastic, etc.—absorb some wavelengths of the visible light spectrum while repelling others. The wavelengths that are not absorbed hit our eyes and are processed by our brains. Imagine a ripe tomato. All colors except shades of Red are absorbed, and the Reds are reflected back to you, as illustrated on page 49.

The **additive** (or RGB) model adds colored lights to make color, like on a TV screen. Remember Isaac Newton's prism theory from Part 1? This model takes it to the next level by controlling the light shown. This is accomplished using just three colors: Red, Green, and Blue. On page 53 is an illustration of how all three colors together make White.

The Sum is the Difference

When my clients contact me for a logo, an ad, a photo, or some other piece of art, they usually say, "Can you send me the file?" This leads me to ask them about the **format** they need… or what medium will be used to publish that art.

Some clients have yet to learn, while others can tell me immediately where they will use it or can provide the specifications. Typically, images are used on multiple channels. The reason why I and other designers ask this is so we can create the correct type of file. Each format follows

different color systems—CMYK for print and RGB for screens. And that's just the beginning.

A Word About Digital Graphics and File Formats

As a business owner, you may receive files in many different formats. I could write a whole chapter on this subject. Basically, there are two types of digital graphics, **vector** and **raster**. Vector graphics are made up of lines and shapes that can be enlarged and reduced without affecting the quality of the image. Vector file formats typically have the following extensions: AI (Adobe Illustrator), EPS (encapsulated postscript), SVG (scalable vector graphics), and PDF (portable document format). These files can be in either the CMYK, RGB or **grayscale** color space. Grayscale, like it says, is shades of Gray or Black. Vector images can also have transparency.

On the other hand, raster files are made up of color pixels. Enlarging these files will cause pixelation. You know what I'm talking about… not pretty. Reducing them could result in a sharper image. Still, it depends on the amount of reduction and how it's being reduced. Raster file formats typically have the following extensions: JPG (or JPEG), BMP, IMG, TIF (or TIFF), GIF, or PNG. GIF and PNG only come as RGBs or grayscale. The rest can be used as any color space. By the way, only GIF and PNG can have a transparent background.

CMYK

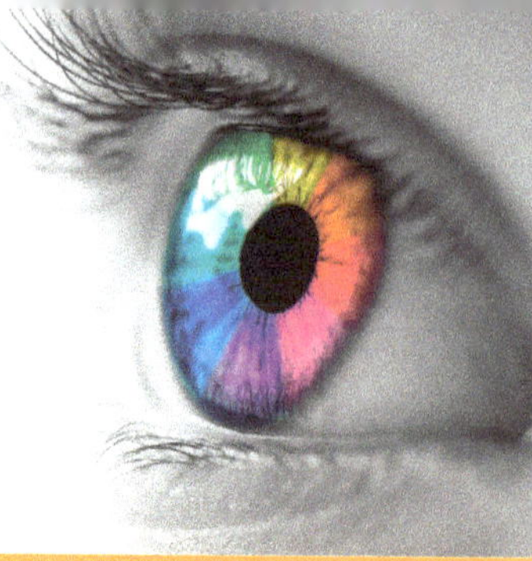

IN PRINT

Absence of color = white or color of material (if other than white)

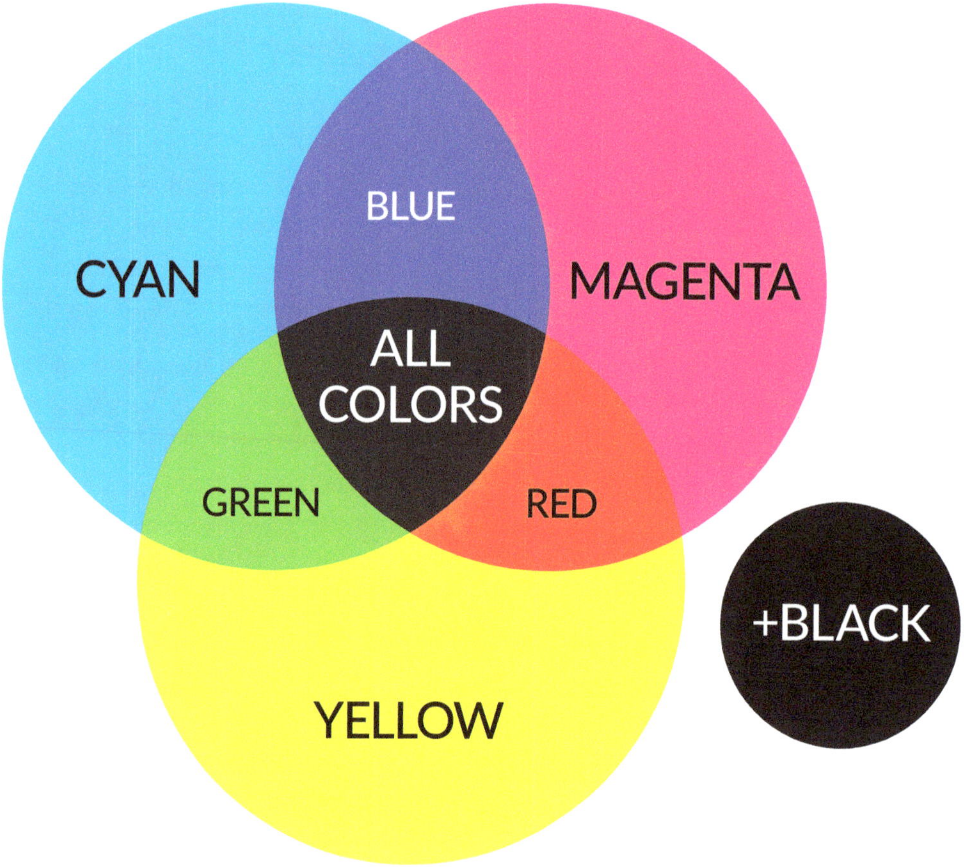

Subtractive Color Systems (in Print)

Don't worry! I'm going to simplify things for you. A subtractive color system, the CMYK color space, is used for printing on paper, billboards, signage, and car wraps. This system includes three primary colors—Cyan, Magenta, and Yellow—plus Black. As subtractive colors, they start with White (or the color of the material—or substrate—that they are being printed on) and absorb (subtract) or reflect colored light wavelengths depending on the color seen. In the example below, a ripe tomato absorbs all colored light wavelengths except the Reds, which are reflected back to us.

CMYK Color Space

As mentioned above, the **CMYK color space** has three primary colors: Cyan (C), Magenta (M), Yellow (Y), plus Black (K). I used to think the K was for the K in Black, but I didn't understand why they couldn't just call it CMYB. Turns out, the K stands for "key" or **key color.** Black is the key color because it is the only way to produce dark, rich tones. Also, the printing industry worried that people would mistake the B for standing for many other colors like Brown, Beige, or Blue. All of which have varying shades, and that would be disastrous. So, K, it is. I know you were wondering the same thing.

CMYK is also called **four-color process,** or just **process color.** With these four ink colors, over a million hues can be made.

Because the CMYK color space is a subtractive system, it must include Black to enrich the dark areas. Yet, it also allows for pure Black text to be printed so that it doesn't always need

to be made up of the three primary colors. In **digital printing**—using a technology that prints directly from an electronic file—this is not as big of a deal because you don't have to worry about **registration** (the process of making all four colors line up properly). But... back in the day, the most common method was **offset printing,** which used large presses with rollers that transferred each color from plates to the paper. Pressmen (the people who ran the presses,

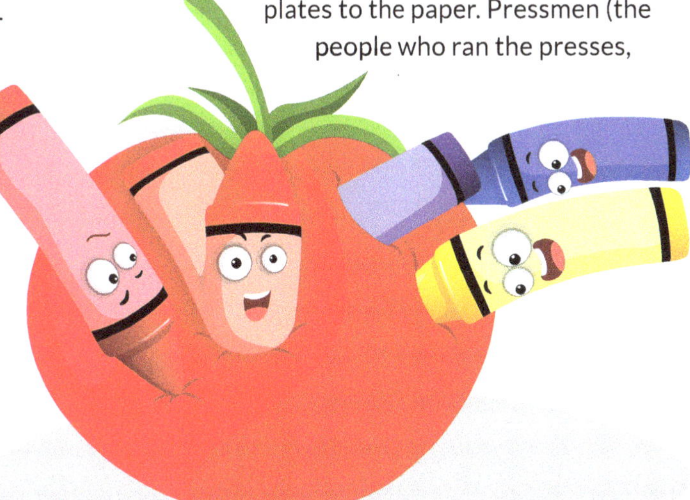

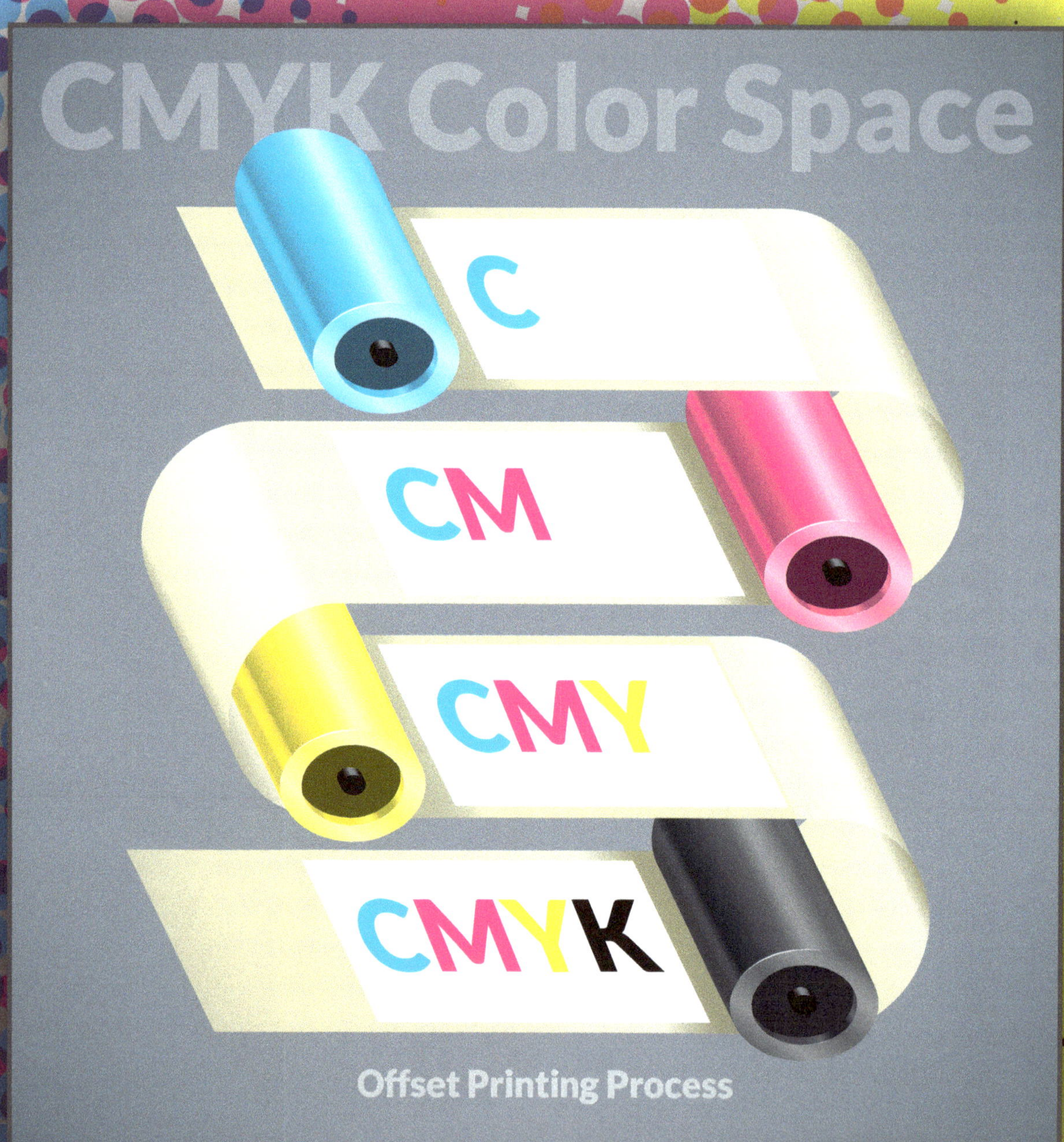
CMYK Color Space
C
CM
CMY
CMYK
Offset Printing Process

like my dad) often wasted a lot of paper just trying to get the ink to register. They required 10% overage in paper for every job.

Offset printing is still used for large runs, especially multi-page documents like newspapers, magazines, and catalogs. But times are changing, and some are being printed digitally more and more. Digital printing allows for variable components that can be costly with offset printing.

Okay, let's talk about another subtractive color model also used in print. Though it is not exactly part of the CMYK color space, it is frequently used in conjunction with it.

Fun Fact: When printing digitally, you can use Rich Black (a combination of all four colors) over Pure Black to get a Black-on-Black or varnished effect. Tell your designer to give it a try on your next project.

Pantone® Matching System

If you've painted a room in your house, you probably went to the paint store and picked out a bunch of swatches. When you narrowed it down to the color you wanted, you gave the number to the paint mixer, who mixed it for you.

The same is true for the Pantone® Matching System (PMS). It is a system of over 5,000 numbered swatches, typically called spot colors in printing. This model is best used for visuals where you only need one or two colors, like promotional products (T-shirts, mugs, tote bags, etc.). By the way, PMS creates the most accurate color matches.

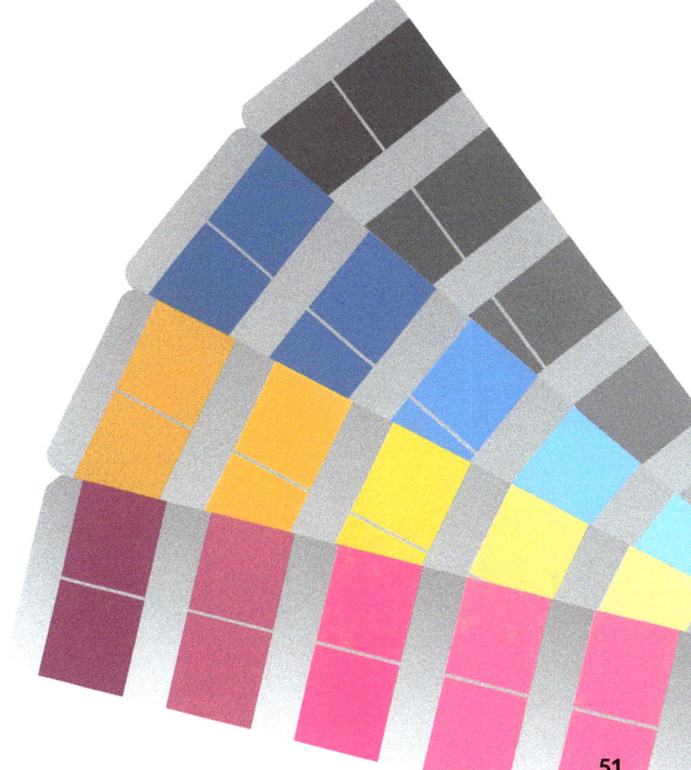

Chapter 5

RGB

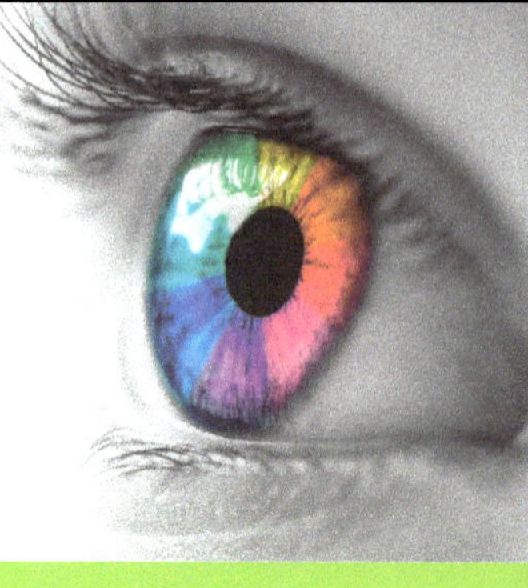

ON SCREEN

Absence of color = black or darkness

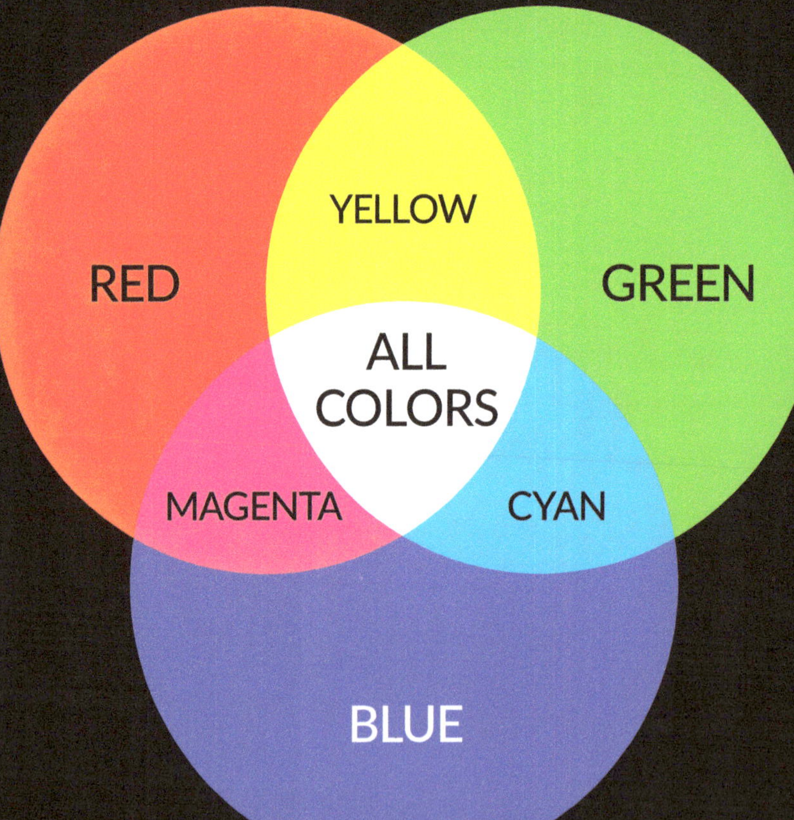

Additive Color Systems (on Screens)

The additive color system uses light in a different way than the subtractive system. It is used for screens (or anything that uses light projection). The colors that you see on your screen are created with light. Each color consists of different variants of these three basic colors: Red, Green, and Blue (RGB)—not to be confused with RBG (Ruth Bader Ginsburg, the late supreme court justice). The more of each color you add, the lighter the color becomes until it is pure White. As you can see in the example below. All three colors projected through your screen become White.

RGB Color Space

When we talk about images on the screen, we use the RGB color space. It combines different intensities of light with the three primary colors to create the visuals that we see on our TV, smartphones, computers, laptops, and more. We use it for images, videos, and anything else that needs to be displayed on the screen.

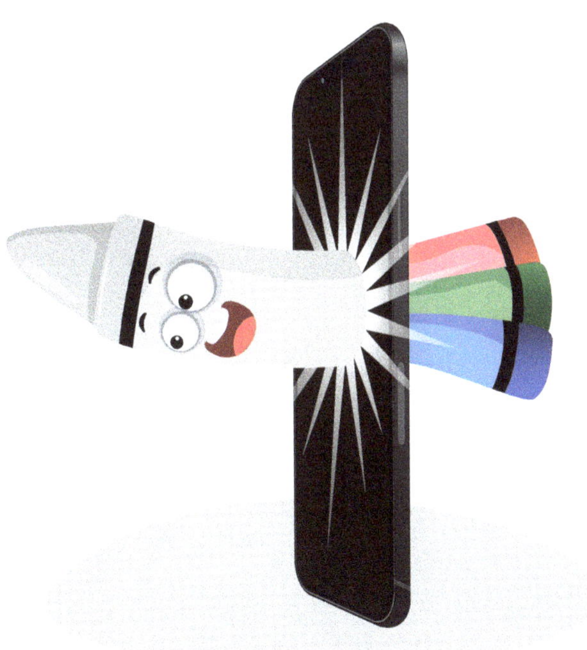

Fun Fact: Any two primary colors from either color space combine to make the primary colors on the other color space. For example, on screen, Red + Blue = Magenta, and, in print, Cyan + Yellow = Green. Interesting, huh?

While CMYK and PMS are for physical printing on a surface, RGB is for computer applications that display with power (electricity) and light used for a website, your social media page, etc. It's the most recognized color system in the world and the most widely used nowadays.

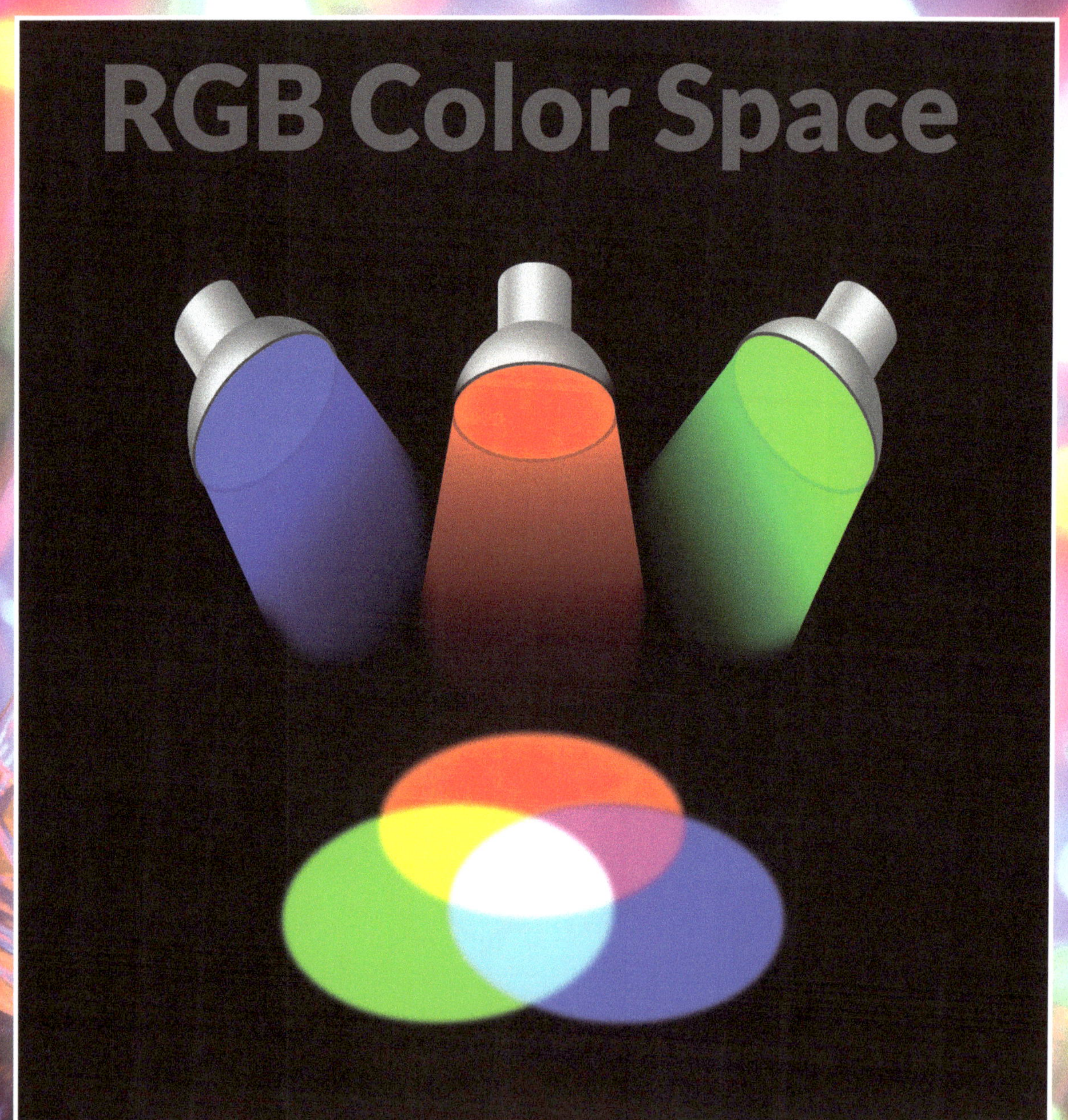
RGB Color Space

You get a whopping 16 million plus colors to choose from with the RGB color space. That's 16 times what you get with CMYK.

Unlike CMYK, RGB uses 256 intensities of each color. In comparison CMYK uses 0%–100% of each color. The 0-255 value system (0 counts as one of the numbers) can get cumbersome. An example would be: R: 255, G: 255, B: 255. A long way to say pure White. (Remember, all colors in the RGB color space make White.) The HEX system was created to simplify this issue.

HEX (Hexadecimal Color)

The **HEX system** is mainly used in web design, although you can use it for other purposes as well. It is basically a hexadecimal representation of the RGB colors. If you don't know the hexadecimal numbers that represent a specific RGB color, just go online and search for an **RGB to HEX converter** or a **CMYK to HEX or RGB converter** or even a **PMS to CMYK converter.** There are a lot of free tools online that can help you, plus you can find some helpful options in the resource section in the back of this book.

Un-Vexing HEX Color

Let's clear up any confusion you may have about HEX color codes. The intensity of each color has been reduced to a pair of number/letter combinations from 0 to 9, then A to F with 0 being no color and F being the highest saturation of color. The first two characters determine the amount of Red, the second set determines Green's intensity, and that leaves Blue's value as the last pair. If all three combinations have identical numbers, i.e. Red has 00, Green has 00, and Blue has 00 then web developers can shorten it to #000 for Black. This shorthand code is mainly used when ALL of the numbers are the same— #000=Black, #FFF=White, or everything in between equals some shade of Gray.

Summing it Up

In Chapter 3, we explored space and the systems that color our world how we see it. We talked about the two predominate color systems, additive and subtractive, along with their purpose. We briefly mentioned RGB and CMYK color spaces. In Chapter 4, we delved into the subtractive system and the color space that goes with it, as well as introducing another color space in the subtractive system. Then, in Chapter 5, we did the same deep dive into the additive system.

What Have You Learned So Far?

Let's test your knowledge about color systems and spaces. Answer the questions below, then compare them to the answer key on page 115 to find out how you did.

1. RGB and CMYK are what's known as

    _________________________________ .

2. What color system uses lightwaves to absorb or reflect light? ________________

3. In the additive color system all lights shining at once, cause what color to be revealed? ___________________________

4. CMYK and HEX are part of the subtractive color system. True or False? ___________

    ____

5. The RGB color space is used to project colors through screens and are a part of the

    ____

    color system.

6. What does CMYK stand for? ___________

    ____

7. The secondary colors in CMYK are the same as the primary colors in RGB and vice versa. True or False? ___________________

8. The Pantone® Matching System or PMS is part of the ___________________

    color system and is best to use as ________ color in printing or___________________

    products such as t-shirts, pens, and mugs which only use one or two colors.

9. What color does #000 make? ___________

10. What is the total number of each color
value in the RGB color space?______________
____

11. What CMYK printing process does this
illustration represent?

____

12. Additive and subtractive are the only two
color systems. True or False? ______________

13. Colors in the RGB color space are reduced
to combinations of number from 0-9 and
letters from ____ to ____ to represent the
intensity of the three colors, _______________,
_______________, and _______________.

14. PMS stands for _______________________
____
____

15. Match the words or acronyms on the left
with the description that best matches it on
the right.

CMYK	System used in print.
RGB	Space used in offset printing.
HEX	System used on screen
Subtractive	Color coding used for websites.
Additive	The most accurate color matches.
Pantone®	Color space with over 16 million color options.

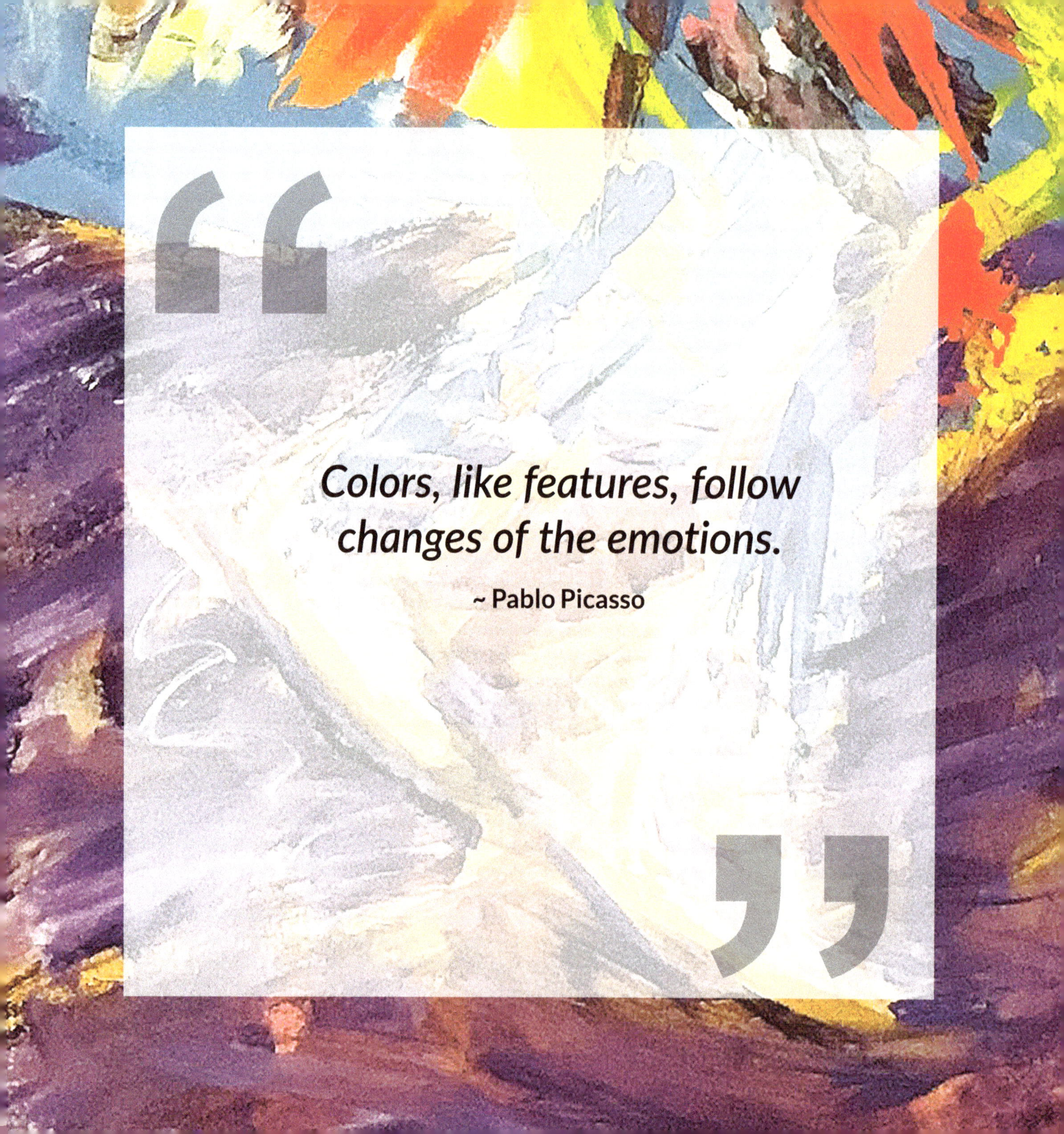
"
Colors, like features, follow
changes of the emotions.
~ Pablo Picasso
"

PART 3: UNDERSTANDING HOW COLOR MAKES US FEEL

[COLOR PSYCHOLOGY]

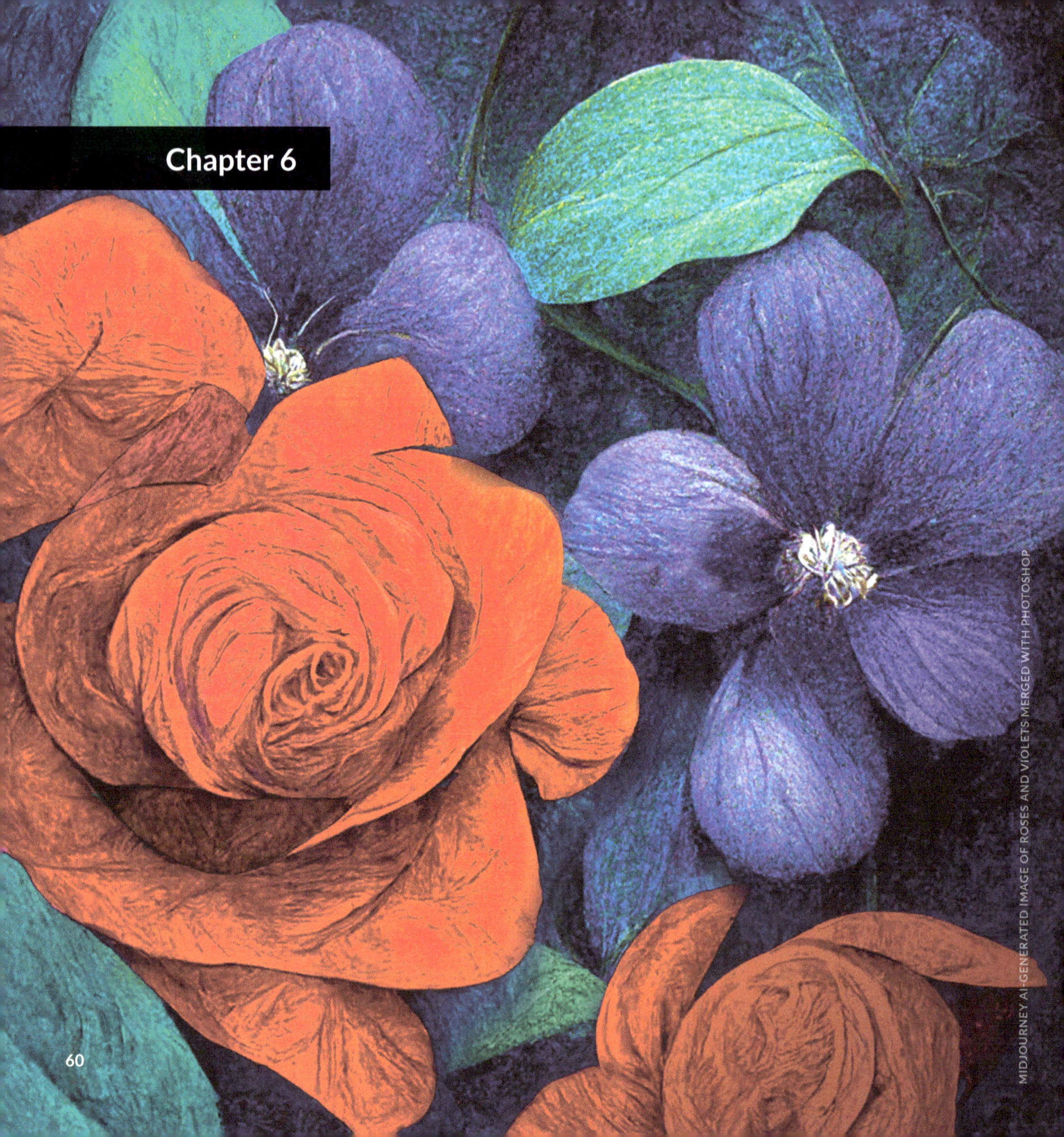

Chapter 6

MIDJOURNEY AI-GENERATED IMAGE OF ROSES AND VIOLETS MERGED WITH PHOTOSHOP

Roses Are Red, Violets Are Blue...

How do you know what color is right for you? You see what I did there? Poetry aside... let's talk about the emotional effects colors can have on us. How do you feel when you enter a Yellow room? Do you prefer a Blue room? What is the color that relaxes you the most? Why do you wear your Green sweatshirt more than your Red one? Artists, scientists, and others have been mesmerized by the effects of colors on our emotions for centuries.

Colors can express a whole variety of actions and physiological reactions. Certain colors that can put a strain on our eyes or increase our blood pressure, which in turn can influence our mood.

Did you know that a color can mean something neutral or special in one culture and mean something totally different in another? The same is true for geographical locations, demographics, and more. How you perceive a specific color might depend on your personal preference, past experiences, culture, or even your gender.

Fun Fact: People can develop a preference or a dislike for a specific color based on emotional experiences they've had with that particular color in their past.

The Influence Color Has on Performance

Have you ever entered an office and immediately felt like something was wrong? Did you ever spend hours finding the right belt, tie, or scarf to go with your outfit? That's your subconscious telling you that the color is wrong for what you plan to do.

Studies have shown that colors have a significant impact on our performance. Just think about your childhood. If you are like me, those big Red markings on your homework were a bit unsettling. Studies have proven that the color Red can actually hurt your performance.

One study conducted in the United States, "Color and psychological functioning: The effect of Red on performance attainment" by Andrew Elliot, Markus Maier, Arlen Moller, Ron Friedman, and Jorg Meinhardt, involved 71 students. Some were given their participant numbers in Red, and others in Black or Green. Seeing the color Red just before an exam had a negative effect on those students' performances.

Color Associations

In Faber Birren's book, *Color Psychology and Color Therapy*, he conducted a survey where people were instructed to say the names of the colors that they associated with different concepts. Here is a sampling of the most popular results:

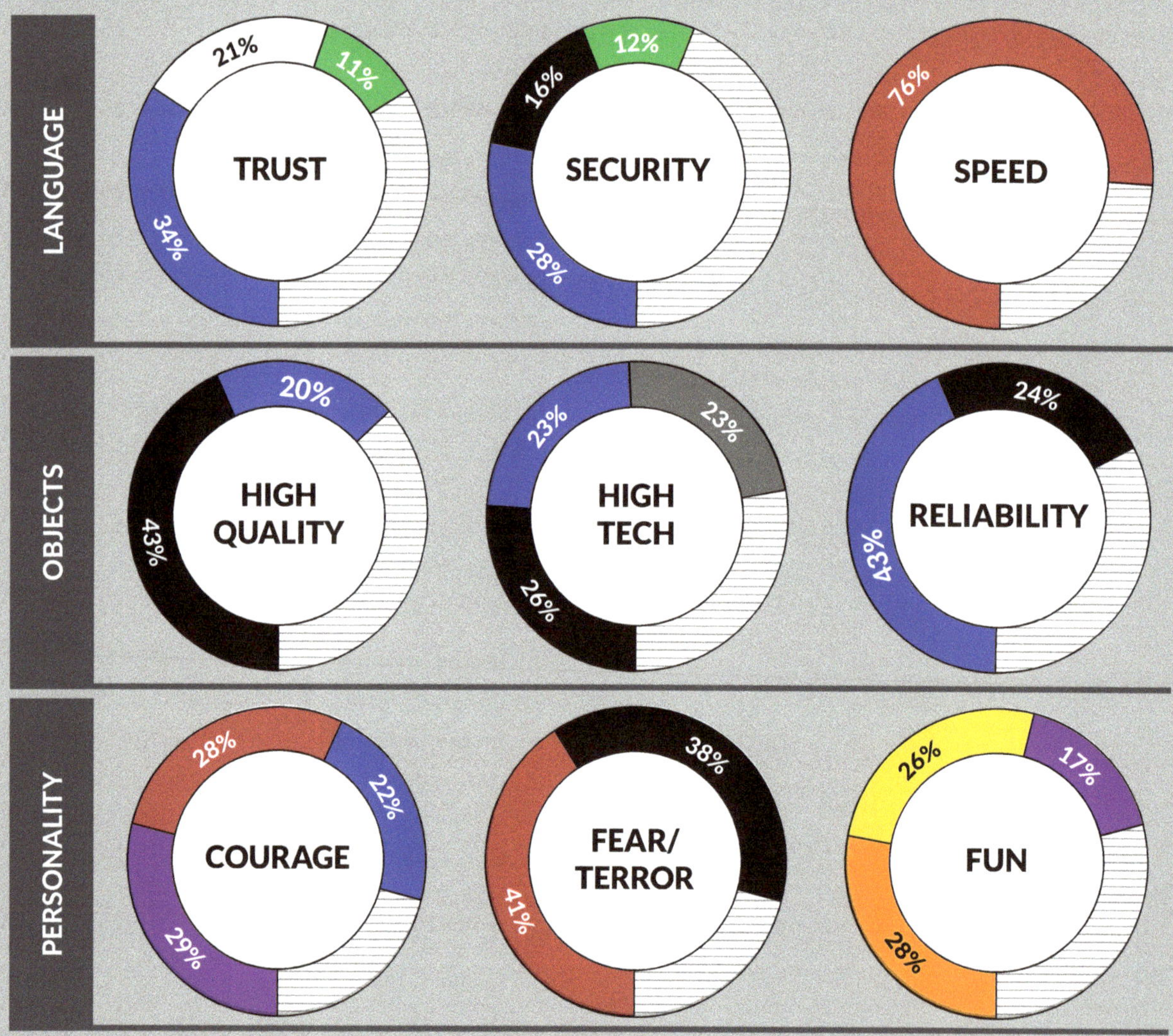

In the mid-twentieth century, author and color researcher Faber Birren published his revolutionary book *Color Psychology and Color Therapy*. He observed that bright colors had a positive effect on "big muscle" activity.

On the other hand, softer colors were better for mental tasks. Birren also found that Blue colors can relax our nerves, while Red often stimulates them. Also, using cooler colors like Green or Blue could enable people to underestimate the passage of time, while using Red and other warm colors tends to make them overestimate the amount of time that has passed.

Birren was not alone in believing that color can be used as therapy. Several cultures, including the ancient Egyptians and the Chinese, used colors to heal. This is called chromotherapy, light therapy, or colorology. It is still used as an alternate, holistic method of treatment today.

What's in a Name?

Although colors have different effects on a person, the color's name is also essential.

In a study published in *Psychology and Marketing* called "A rose by any other name..." the recipients were given makeup products with the same colors but different names. According to the results, participants pre-ferred products with "fancy" color names. For instance, they preferred the color "Mocha" rather than "Brown" even though they were the same exact color. And it's not just makeup products; people just prefer creative names for colors for just about anything.

Color Coordination for Customer Conversions (That's a lot of C words)

The Internet is full of blogs and articles about color psychology and choosing the right color for your branding, including your website and logo, to get the most conversions. Although these articles make some good points, the fact is that there is no single color that will do the trick for you.

There's a principle of psychology called the **isolation effect.** Let me just tell you what it means without going into too much detail. This principle states that if something stands out like a sore thumb, it will be remembered more than others. For example, in a HubSpot blog article written by Joshua Porter, they ran an **A/B test** (a marketing technique that compares two versions of a web page or application to see which performs better, also known as **split testing**), where Perfomable tested their regular Green brand color against Red for their **CTA** (call-to-action) button on their website when Red wasn't even a part of their brand. The conversion rate for the Red button was 21% higher than the Green button.

Chapter 7

Romantic or Aggressive

Playful or Uncomfortable

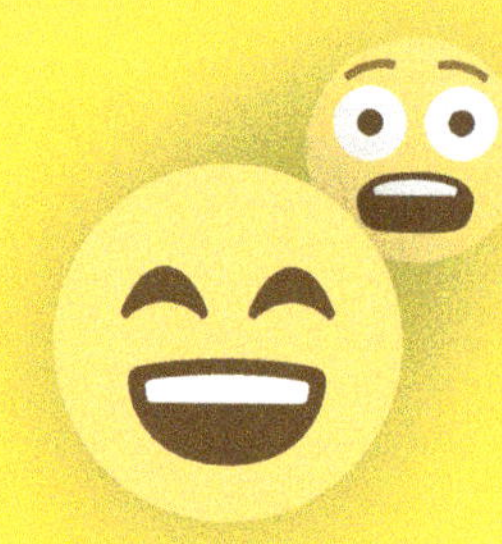

Joy or Fear

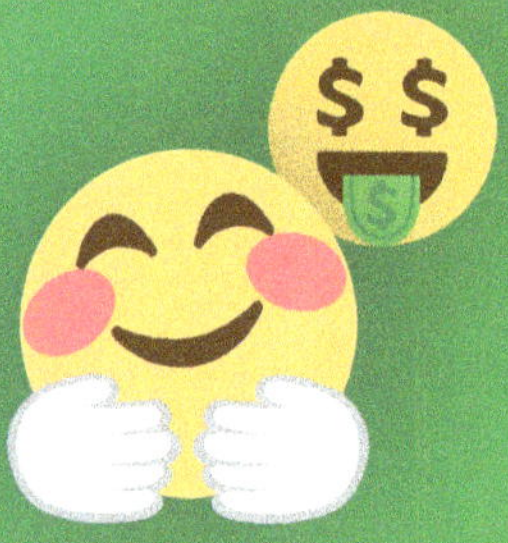

Peaceful or Greedy

Trusting or Worried

Spiritual or Moody

Pure or Empty

Sophisticated or Depressed

Down-to-Earth or Unsophisticated

The Good, The Bad, and The Different

Colors can have both positive and negative effects on people's brains. So, being aware of both sides can save you from trouble down the road. For instance, if your target audience tends to have anger issues, you may not want to use Red as your primary color. Similarly, suppose you are targeting a sophisticated audience. In that case, you may want to avoid using Brown in your color palette unless your brand has something to do with chocolate. There are also cultural differences that could come into play.

On the following two pages, I have two charts that show symbols of the effects represented throughout this chapter. Take time to follow the instructions to help you find your brand colors. Now, let's have some fun. Let's look at some color categories and check out the potential positive, negative, or cultural effects they can have on us as consumers.

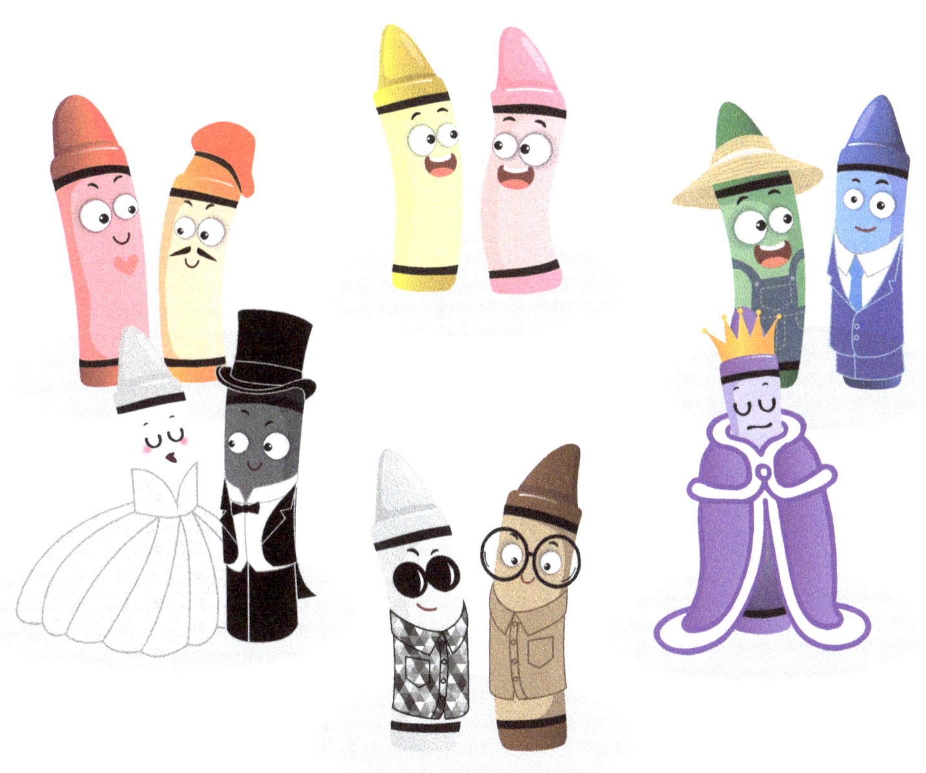

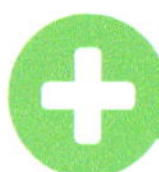

Glamorous
Luxurious
Nobel
Royalty
Wealthy
Elegant
Sophistication

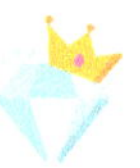

Acceptance
Connection
Dependability
Loyalty
Reliability
Trusted
Trustworthy

Faithful
Femininity
Love
Passionate
Romance
Sensitivity
Trusting
Vulnerability

Fun
Hopeful
Joyful
Playful
Youthful
Openness
Clarity
Truth Seeking

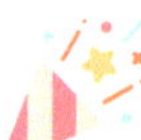

Alive
Down to Earth
Freshness
Growth
Health
Natural
Wellness
Vitality
Earthiness

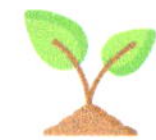

Authority
Boldness
Confident
Credibility
Durability
Powerful
Strong

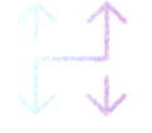

Neutrality
Versatility
Universality

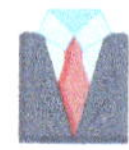

Conservative
Intelligent
Nostalgic
Professional
Seriousness
Traditional
Wisdom

Action
Brave
Courageous
Energy
Excitement

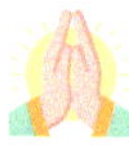

Calming
Charity
Harmony
Nurturing
Peaceful
Relaxed
Spiritual
Purity
Serenity
Soothing

Approachability
Friendliness
Happiness
Innocence
Kindness
Sweetness

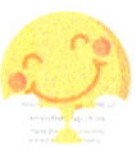

Comfort
Encouragement
Positivity
Warmth

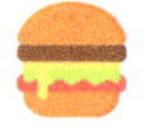

Appetite-
Stimulating
Appealing
Cravable

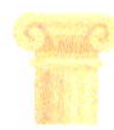

Classic
Modern
Timelessness

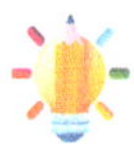

Creative
Innovative
Imagination
Uniqueness

Intrigue
Mystery
Mystique

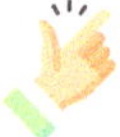

Simplicity
Minimalism

Attention-Grabbing
Emphasis
Contrast
Stand Out

Caution
Danger
Warning

Aggression
Defiance
Intimidation
Trouble

Fatigue
Jaundice
Overwhelm
Over-stimulation
Sickening

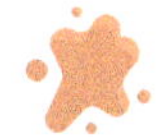

Dirty
Unpleasantness
Muddiness
Unsophisticated

Blandness
Dullness
Indistinctness
Stagnation
Lackluster

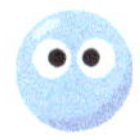

Coldness
Depression
Emotionless
Introversion
Sadness
Sterility

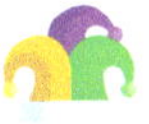

Cheapness
Immaturity
Frivolity
Simple-minded

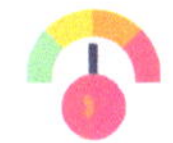

Commonality
Limited
Predictability

Elitism
Exclusivity
High Maintenance
Isolation
Oppression

Cowardice
Envy
Greed
Jealousy
Hate

Darkness
Death
Fear
Too Mysterious

Eccentricity
Oddity
Quirky
Somberness
Twisted

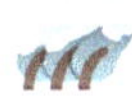

Heaviness
Intensity
Moodiness

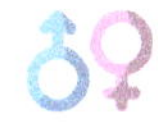

Gender
Emasculating
Stereotypes

Before moving on...

Circle the symbols on the page to the left that most represent the feelings you want your brand to convey. Then, circle the symbols above that your brand will definitely need to avoid based on your target audience. These are the symbols you'll want to look for throughout this chapter. Keep in mind that's it's not an exact science and is somewhat subjective.

DISCLAIMER: *Your symbol may not be on the color you want. That doesn't mean it doesn't convey the feelings you want. They just aren't the strongest for that color. It's not all carved in stone. Trust me. These are guidelines, but consider what is more important to you... having the color you want even though it doesn't strongly evoke the emotions you want to convey or having a color that will.*

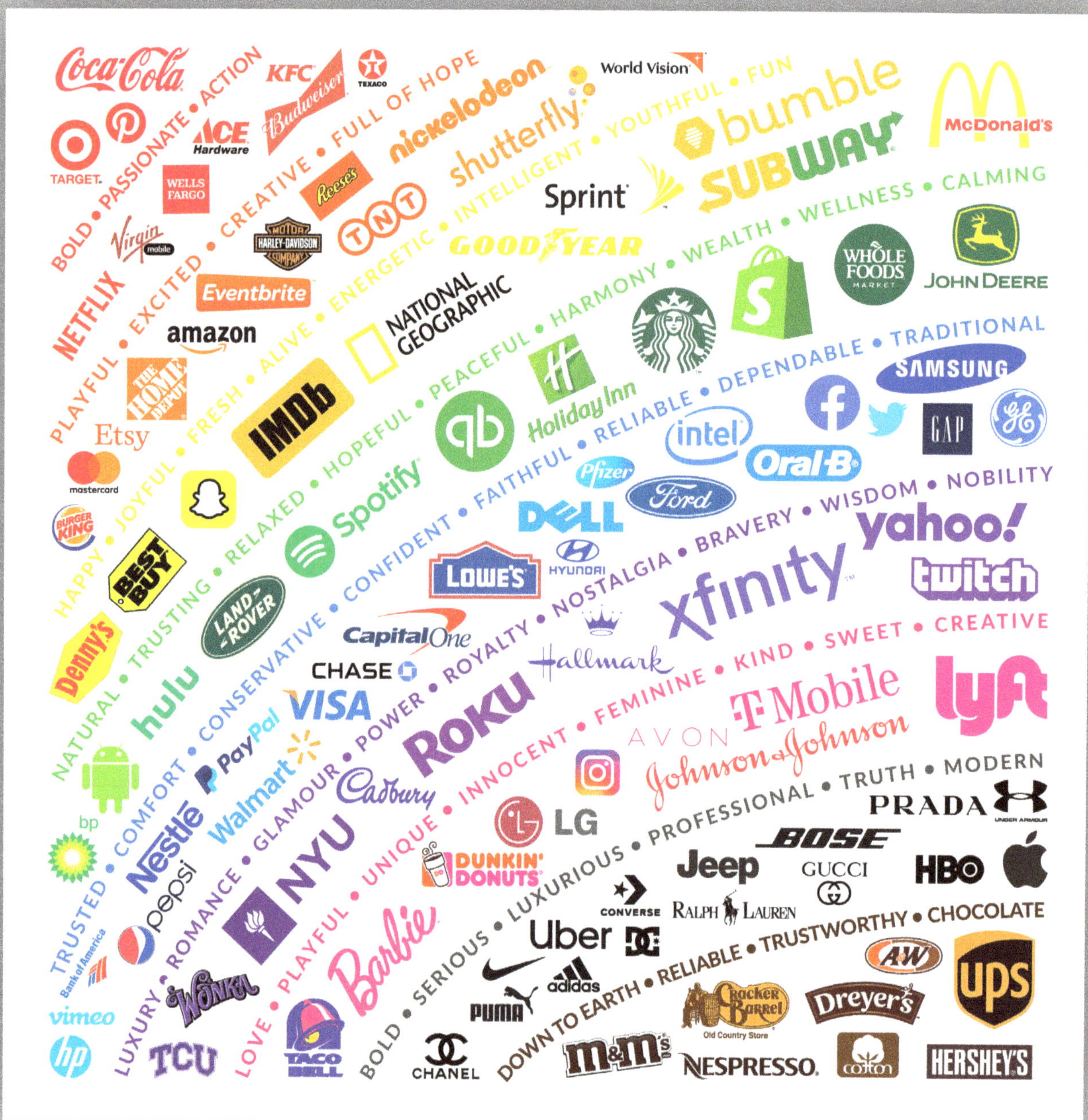

REDs

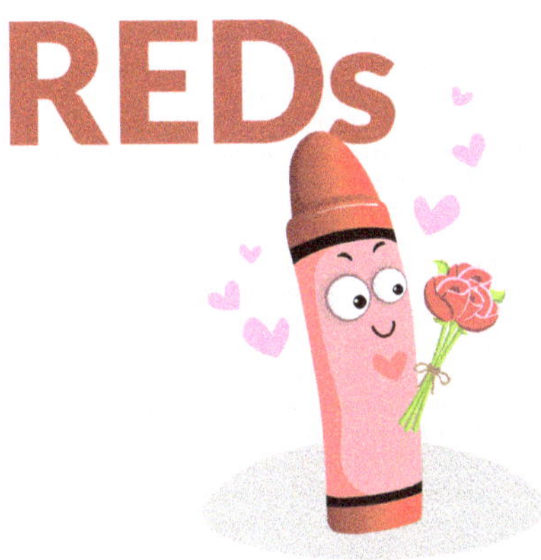

REDs capture our *attention*. Red is associated with *energy, passion,* and *action* making it perfect for CTAs (call-to-action phrases and buttons) on websites, social media channels, etc. Red is one of the most intense colors in any palette and provokes the strongest emotions.

Did you know Red can also *enhance appetite*? That is one of the reasons why fast-food restaurants use it in their branding, marketing, and decor. If your brand is a restaurant or food, you may want to consider Red as part of your palette. Hmm, now I'm hungry.

POTENTIALLY POSITIVE EFFECTS

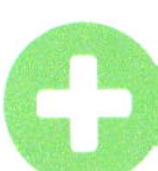 *Attention-Grabbing:* Red has a strong visual impact and can stand out in a crowded marketplace, creating a memorable impression.

 *Energy and Excitement:* Red can evoke enthusiasm and urgency, stimulating consumer interest.

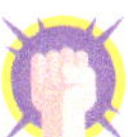 *Boldness and Confidence:* Red can convey a sense of confidence, power, and authority, projecting strength and dominance.

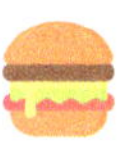 *Appetite Stimulation:* Red can increase food cravings, making it popular in the food and beverage industry, particularly with fast food.

POTENTIALLY NEGATIVE EFFECTS

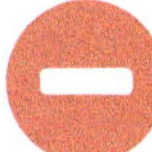 *Aggression or Intimidation:* Red can sometimes be associated with aggression, intensity, or danger, creating a sense of alarm.

 *Overwhelmed and Fatigued:* Red's intensity can be overwhelming if used excessively. Prolonged exposure to Red may lead to visual fatigue. Balance its usage for visual harmony.

SOME CULTURAL DIFFERENCES

The meaning and associations of Red can vary across different regions and cultures. In some cultures, Red may symbolize luck, celebration, or vitality. In contrast, it may represent danger and other negative connotations in other cultures. You should consider these cultural nuances if your brand has an international presence.

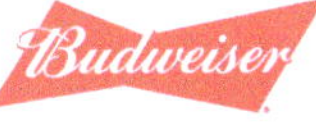
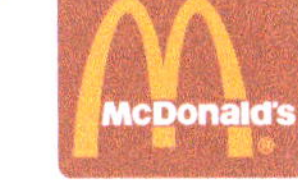
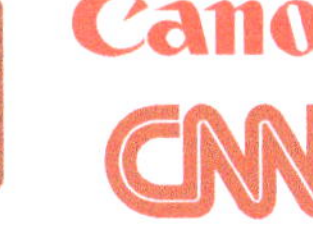
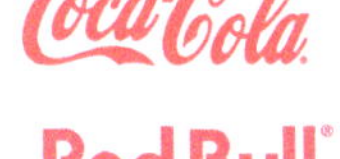

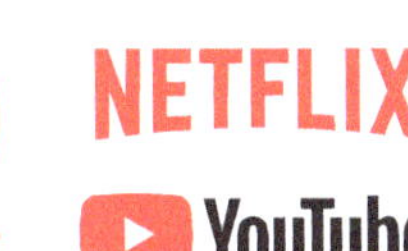
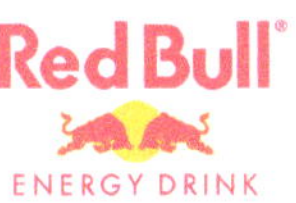

ORANGEs

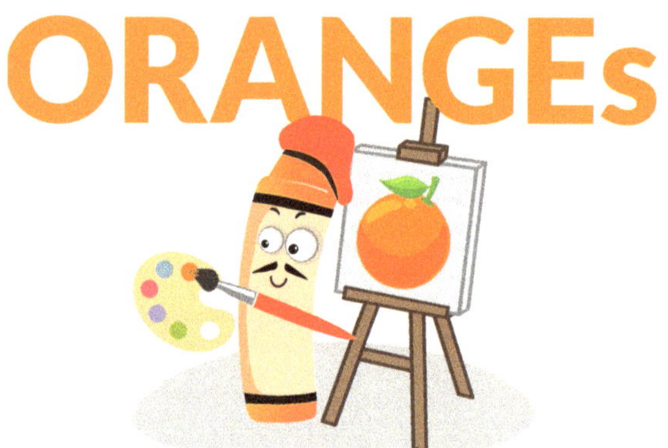

The minute I see **ORANGEs**, I feel *excited, creative,* and *energetic.* How about you? Orange can also make you feel *adventurous, hopeful,* and *playful.*

Orange doesn't command attention as much as Red, but it's still very eye-catching. **Nickelodeon** is a channel for kids, and the Orange in its brand can get children excited. Many creative, adventurous people go to **Home Depot** to get supplies for DIY projects. I'm exhausted just thinking about it.

POTENTIALLY POSITIVE EFFECTS

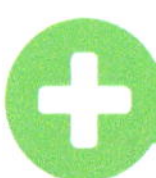

Energy and Excitement: Orange can evoke feelings of energy and excitement, creating a vibrant and lively brand image.

Creativity and Innovation: Orange is associated with creativity and innovation. It can inspire imaginative thinking and originality.

Approachability and Friendliness: Orange is a friendly and approachable color. It can create a welcoming and inviting atmosphere, fostering community and connection.

Stand Out: Orange is a less common brand color choice than Blue or Red, but using it can differentiate brands and capture attention in a distinct way.

POTENTIALLY NEGATIVE EFFECTS

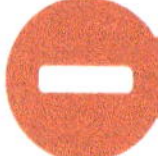

Over-stimulation or Discomfort: Energetic and attention-grabbing colors like Orange can become overwhelming and cause people to feel uncomfortable if used excessively.

Immaturity or Cheapness: In some contexts, Orange may be associated with cheap or low-quality products.

SOME CULTURAL DIFFERENCES

Like other colors, the cultural associations of Orange can vary across different regions and cultures. It may have different meanings and connotations, such as celebration or spirituality. Brands with an international presence should be mindful of these cultural nuances.

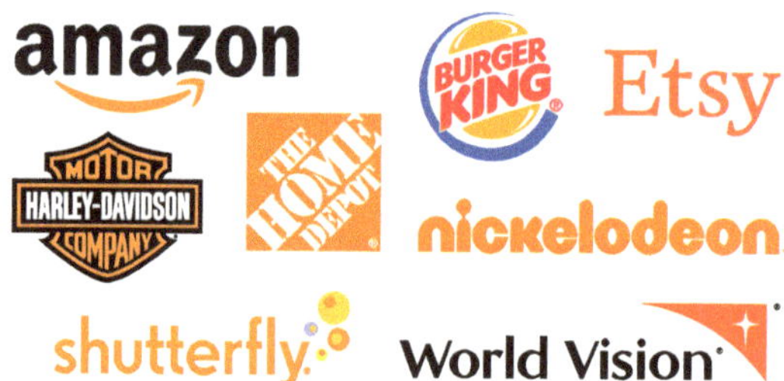

YELLOWs

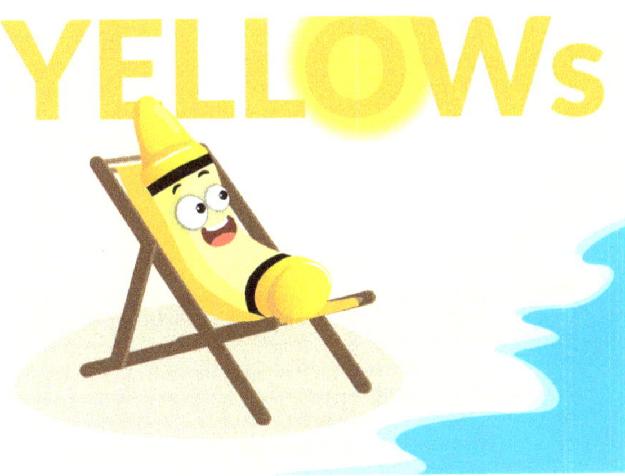

Sunny days make me *happy* if it's not too hot. I live in Texas! **YELLOWs,** of course, are typically associated with a sunny day. But feeling happy can have other effects on brands.

Ever wonder how you feel so good about eating your favorite meal at a restaurant like **McDonald's?** Well, you know that McDonald's and others use Red to enhance their customers' appetites. They use Yellow to make them feel good about it. Maybe that's why there are so many fast-food restaurants that use the Red and Yellow color combination.

POTENTIALLY POSITIVE EFFECTS

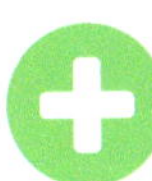

Positivity and Happiness: Yep, Yellow is often associated with positivity and happiness. It evokes feelings of joy, energy, and enthusiasm, creating a cheerful and uplifting image.

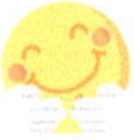

Attention-Grabbing: Yellow is highly visible and can catch the viewer's attention quickly, grab people's eyes and create a memorable impression.

Warmth and Friendliness: Yellow is considered a warm and friendly color, creating a welcoming and approachable atmosphere that fosters a sense of openness and connection.

POTENTIALLY NEGATIVE EFFECTS

Overstimulation or Fatigue: Yellow is a bright and intense color. While it can be attention-grabbing, prolonged exposure to it or excessive use of it may cause visual fatigue or overstimulation. It's important to use Yellow strategically and balance it with other colors to maintain visual harmony.

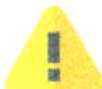

Caution or Warning: In some contexts, Yellow may be associated with caution or warning signs. Brands should be cautious when using Yellow to avoid any unintended negative connotations, especially in industries where safety is a primary concern.

SOME CULTURAL DIFFERENCES

Like other colors, the cultural associations of Yellow can vary across different regions and cultures. It may have different meanings and connotations, such as wealth, happiness, or cowardice. Brands with an international presence should consider these cultural nuances.

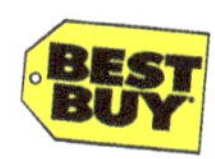
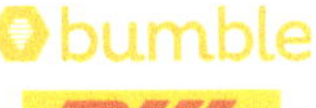
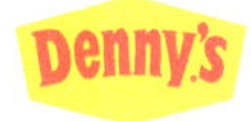

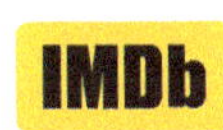
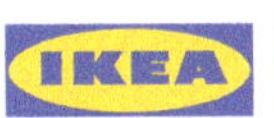
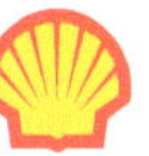
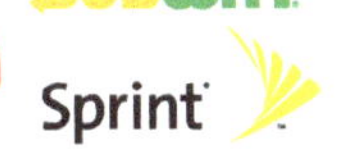

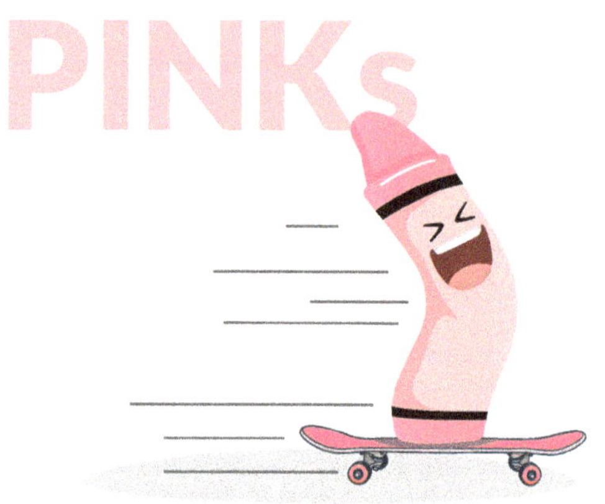

PINKs

At one time **PINKs** were synonymous with girls. It can still represent *femininity* but also *playfulness*, *youth*, and *unconditional love*.

Today, Pink is not just used for products marketed to girls, like Barbie. You can see brands like T-Mobile and Lyft using the playful and youthful qualities of the color Pink in their marketing campaigns. These brands cater to all genders. In the current gender climate, the norms are blurred, so why not mix things up?

POTENTIALLY POSITIVE EFFECTS

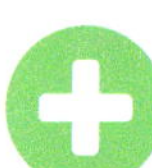
Femininity and Sensitivity: Pink is associated with femininity, sensitivity, and nurturing, evoking feelings of tenderness, care, and compassion, to convey a soft and gentle image.

Playfulness and Youthfulness: Playfulness, youthfulness, and innocence can create a light-hearted and fun atmosphere.

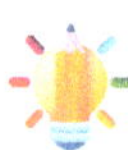
Uniqueness and Creativity: Using Pink can make your brand stand out from the competition and create a unique identity.

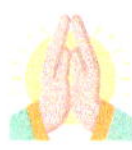
Calming and Soothing: Certain shades of Pink, such as pastel or muted tones, can have a calming and soothing effect.

POTENTIALLY NEGATIVE EFFECTS

Gender Stereotypes: Pink is often associated with gender stereotypes, particularly femininity. While this can be a positive quality in some contexts, it may limit the appeal to a specific gender or reinforce stereotypes.

Immaturity or Frivolity In some contexts, Pink may be associated with immaturity or frivolity. Brands targeting a mature or sophisticated audience may avoid Pink to maintain a more serious or professional image.

SOME CULTURAL DIFFERENCES

Pink's meaning and cultural associations can vary across different regions and cultures. It may have different meanings, such as love, sweetness, or femininity. Brands with an international presence should be mindful of these cultural nuances.

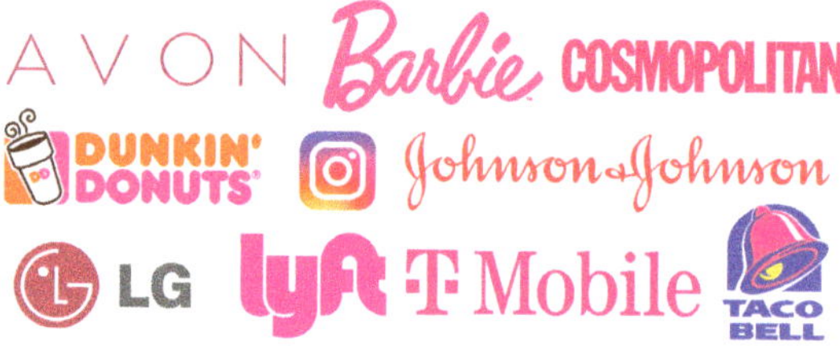

GREENs

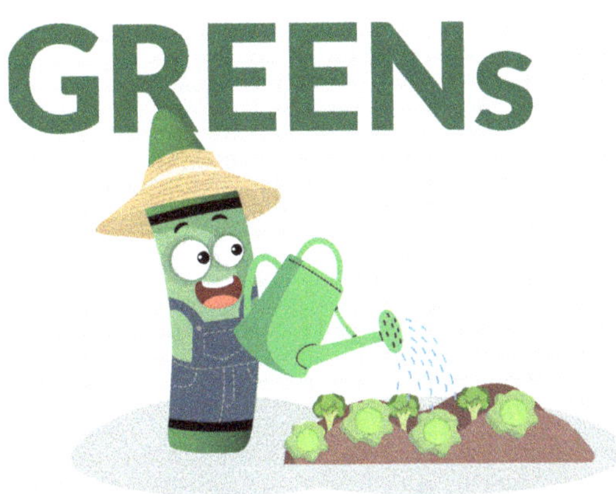

Besides being my favorite color, the first thing that comes to my mind when thinking about Green is typically one of two things: money or nature. **GREENs** are associated with both. It also represents health, wealth, fertility, growth, and generosity.

Health product brands such as **Whole Foods** tend to choose one or more shades/tints of Green as their main color(s). Of course, other industries that pertain to money and nature use Green in their branding, like banking (**Chime**) and agriculture (**John Deere**).

POTENTIALLY POSITIVE EFFECTS

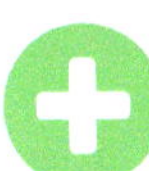
Nature and Freshness: Nature, growth, and freshness are the epitome of Green, evoking feelings of harmony, balance, and renewal.

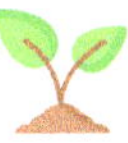
Relaxation and Calmness: Green has a calming effect and is often associated with relaxation and tranquility, calmness, and serenity.

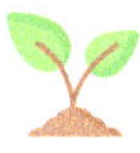
Health and Vitality: Green is also associated with health, vitality, and abundance. It can convey a sense of well-being, energy, and life.

POTENTIALLY NEGATIVE EFFECTS

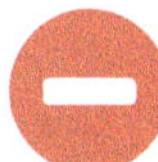
Envy or Jealousy: Green can sometimes be associated with envy or jealousy.

Blandness or Stagnation: Green can be perceived as bland or stagnant. Use creatively or in combination with other colors.

SOME CULTURAL DIFFERENCES

The meaning and cultural associations of Green can vary across different regions and cultures. In some cultures, Green may symbolize luck, fertility, or money, while in others, it may have different meanings or connotations. Brands with an international presence should consider these cultural nuances.

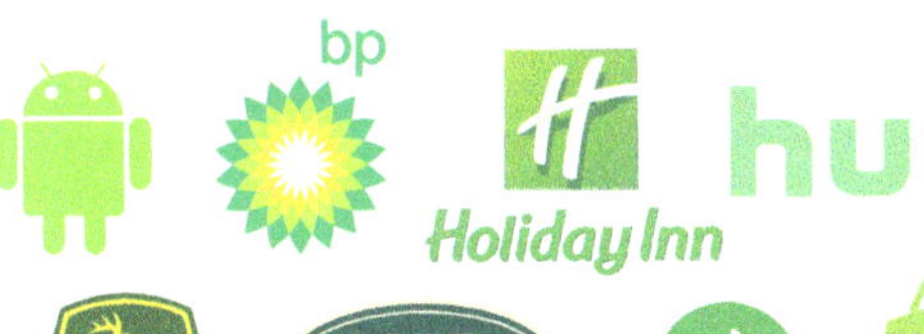
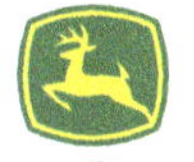
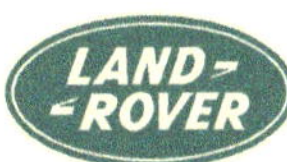

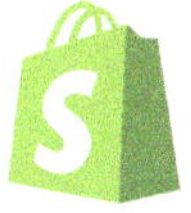
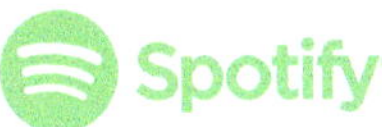
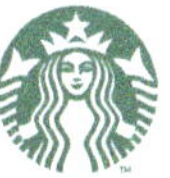
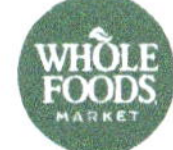

BLUEs

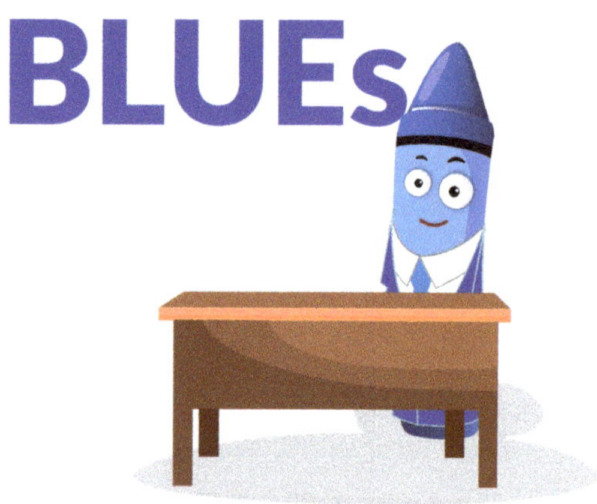

BLUEs are associated with the color of the sky and water. They represent *peace, harmony, stability, calm,* and *trust.* That is why finance-related brands like **CapitalOne** and **Bank of America** choose Blue as one of their official colors in branding strategies.

It may not surprise you, but Blue is the most popular brand color. Tech brands such as **Meta, Twitter,** and **Intel** use this color in their marketing campaigns to promote *loyalty.* While retailers like **Walmart** and health brands like **Oral B** use Blue to enhance the brand's *trustworthiness* and *reliability.*

POTENTIALLY POSITIVE EFFECTS

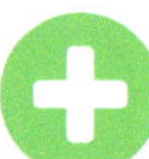
Trust and Reliability: Blue is associated with trust, reliability, and professionalism, conveying a sense of security and stability.

Calmness and Serenity: Blue has a calming effect and can create a sense of serenity, promoting a relaxed and peaceful experience.

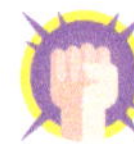
Authority and Credibility: By projecting an image of authority and credibility, Blue helps to establish a positive reputation and leadership.

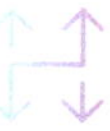
Universality and Acceptance: As a universally accepted color, Blue is less likely to evoke negative cultural associations.

POTENTIALLY NEGATIVE EFFECTS

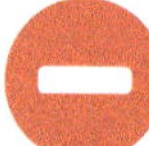
Lack of Excitement: Blue can be perceived as lacking excitement or energy, It may not convey a sense of vibrancy or playfulness.

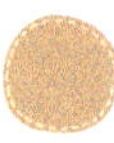
Coldness and Sterility: Since Blue can evoke feelings of coldness or sterility, opt for warmer colors to create a more engaging atmosphere

Commonality and Predictability: Blue is a popular color choice for brands, which means it can be perceived as predictable or generic.

SOME CULTURAL DIFFERENCES

While Blue is an internationally safe color for brands, their are a few cultural nuances to consider. For instance, In some cultures Blue is used for protection or to ward off evil spirits. It can also be associated with spirituality, faith, devotion, or divinity.

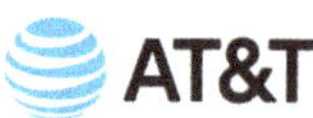
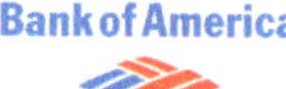
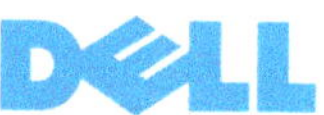
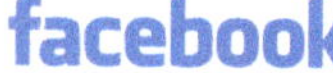
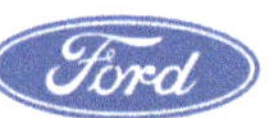
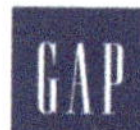
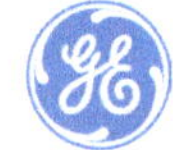
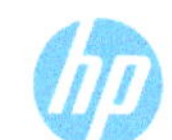
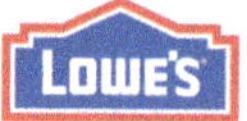
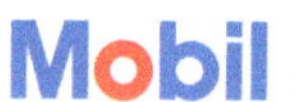
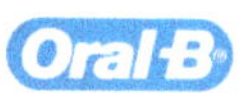
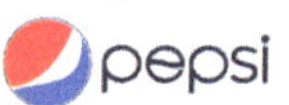
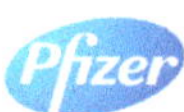
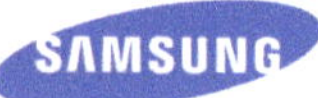
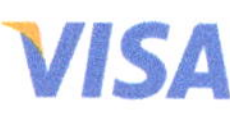

PURPLEs

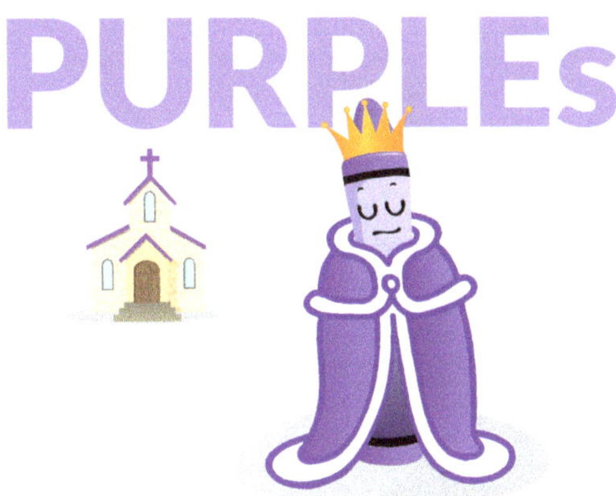

PURPLEs have been associated with royalty for as long as I can remember. There was a time when only nobles and royals were allowed to wear Purple. In those times, wearing Purple was the same as wearing jewelry. Today, it's associated with *power, nobility, luxury, wisdom, and spirituality.*

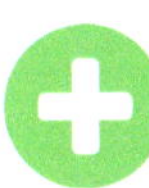 POTENTIALLY POSITIVE EFFECTS

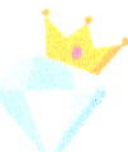 *Royalty and Luxury:* Purple has historically been associated with royalty, luxury, and nobility. It can convey a sense of elegance, sophistication, and exclusivity, which is ideal for targeting upscale markets.

Creativity and Imagination: Purple is often associated with creativity, imagination, and spirituality. It can inspire artistic thinking and evoke a sense of individuality.

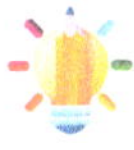 *Mystery and Intrigue:* Purple can create an aura of mystery, depth, and intrigue. It is often used to pique curiosity and build a sense of allure.

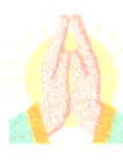 *Calming and Spiritual:* Certain shades of Purple, such as lavender or lilac, can be calming and soothing. They are associated with spirituality, relaxation, and mindfulness.

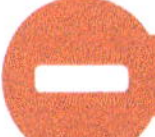 POTENTIALLY NEGATIVE EFFECTS

 *Exclusivity or Elitism:* While Purple can convey a sense of luxury and exclusivity, it may also be perceived as elitist or inaccessible by some audiences. Those targeting a broader or more inclusive demographic may need to balance Purple with other colors to maintain relatability.

 *Somberness or Eccentricity:* In certain contexts, darker shades of Purple can evoke a somber or melancholic atmosphere. Additionally, bright or bold Purples may be seen as eccentric or unconventional.

 SOME CULTURAL DIFFERENCES

The meaning and cultural associations of Purple can vary across different regions and cultures. It may symbolize different things, such as wealth, spirituality, or mourning, depending on the cultural context. Brands with an international presence should be aware of these cultural nuances.

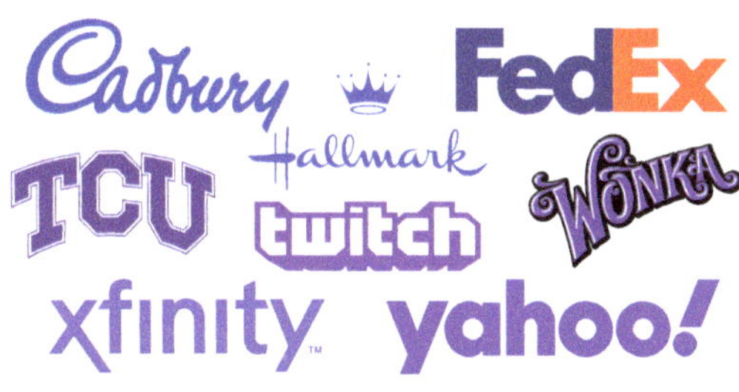

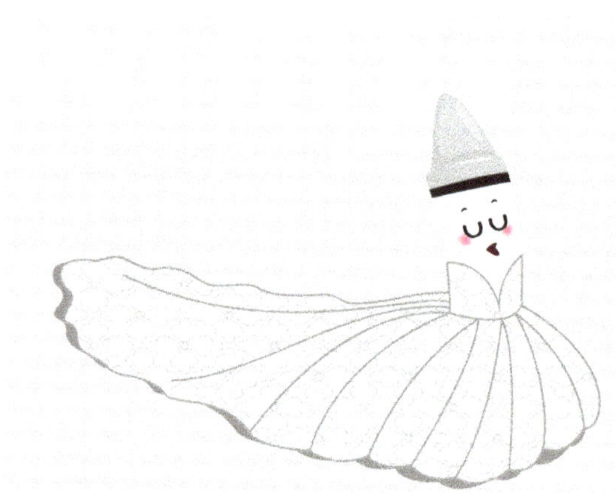

In some cultures, **WHITEs** are associated with *innocence, purity, and goodness.* For example, in the U.S., only the bride is allowed to wear White on their wedding day to signify *purity.*

Just keep in mind that it could differ in other cultures. In some parts of the world, White has the opposite meaning.

FedEx uses the White space in its logo between the "E" and "X" to create an arrow which represents transportation and speed.

POTENTIALLY POSITIVE EFFECTS

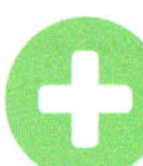
Purity and Simplicity: White is associated with purity, cleanliness, and simplicity. It can convey a sense of clarity and freshness, projecting a clean and sleek image.

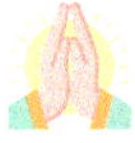
Versatility and Neutrality: White is a versatile and neutral color that complements other colors to create a sense of balance. It serves as a backdrop, allowing content to take center stage.

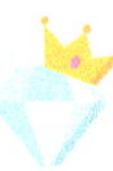
Sophistication and Timelessness: White can convey a sense of sophistication, elegance, and timelessness, often associated with luxury and high-end brands.

Openness and Clarity: White has a visually open and spacious quality, creating a sense of clarity, and transparency. White can convey a sense of accessibility or purity of intention.

POTENTIALLY NEGATIVE EFFECTS

Lack of Distinctiveness: White, a common and neutral color, may lack distinctiveness and struggle to stand out independently.

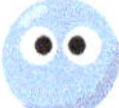
Sterility or Coldness: In specific contexts, an excessive use of White can create a sterile or cold atmosphere.

High Maintenance: White can be challenging to maintain and keep clean, especially in practical applications.

SOME CULTURAL DIFFERENCES

In some cultures White is associated with mourning and death. It is worn at funerals and symbolizes grieving and the cycle of life. White can be related to peace, surrender, and tranquility. Some cultures revere White as holy and spiritual, representing divine qualities, and it is often used in religious rituals and ceremonies.

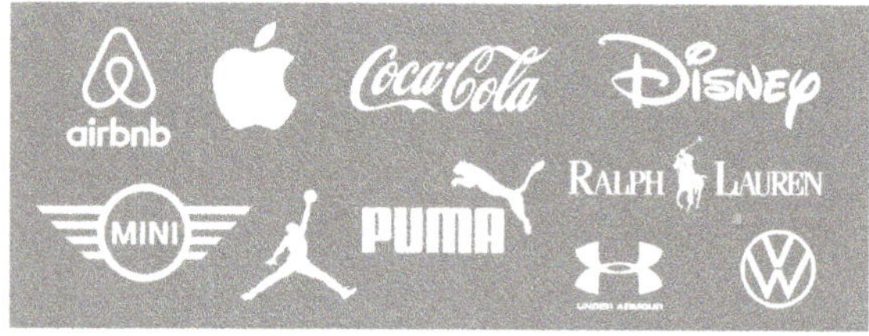

BLACKs

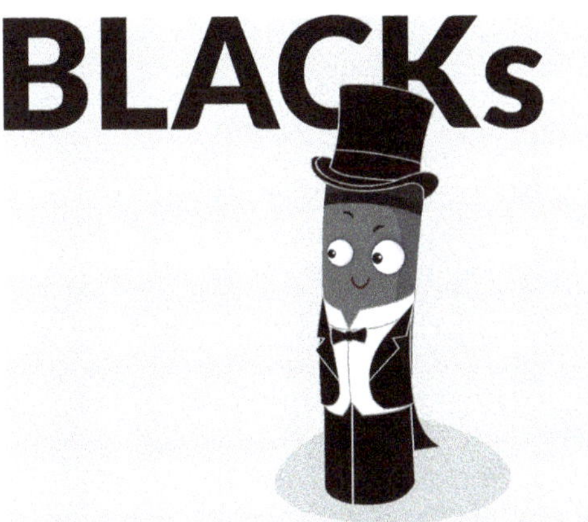

BLACKs have a classic sophistication. Black's *timeless* appeal makes it extremely *versatile.* In fact, most, if not all brands, use Black in text and backgrounds for *readability.* But, as a brand color, Black can evoke feelings of *influence, power,* and *authority.* On the down side, Black can also represent *mystery, darkness, sadness* and *anger.*

In some cultures, Black is used to represent *death* and in other cultures, it can be the exact opposite.

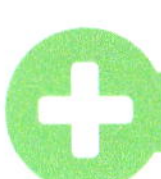
Elegance and Sophistication: Black is often associated with elegance, sophistication, and luxury, conveying a sense of prestige and exclusivity.

Timelessness and Classic Appeal: Black is a timeless color that is always in style, creating a sense of longevity for a brand.

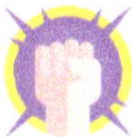
Strength and Power: Black can convey strength, authority, and power. Its commanding presence creates a sense of confidence.

Contrast and Emphasis: Black is a strong contrast color, allowing other elements to stand out and grab attention. It can create visual impact and enhance the visibility of certain colors or design elements.

Intensity and Heaviness: Black can be perceived as intense and heavy, mainly when used extensively or inappropriately, creating a severe or somber atmosphere.

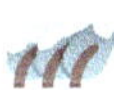
Connotations of Mystery or Darkness: Black is often associated with mystery, darkness, or the unknown, potentially creating negative connotations or misconceptions.

Lack of Vibrancy: Black, being a dark and neutral color, may lack vibrancy or dynamism on its own.

While many cultures associate black with grief and mourning, some associate Black with mystery, power, and the unknown. Black can symbolize the depths of the subconscious or represent authority and strength.

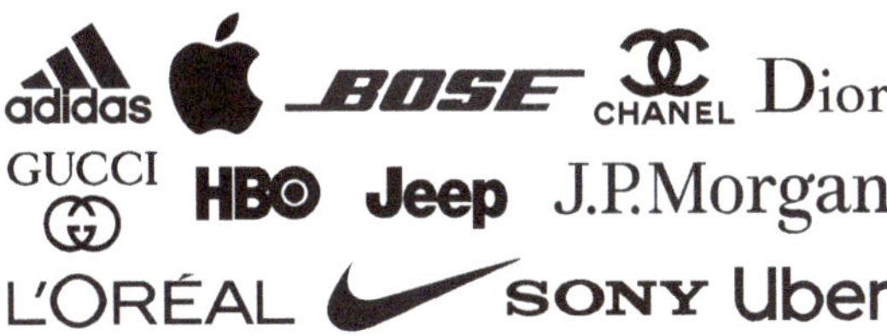

GRAYs

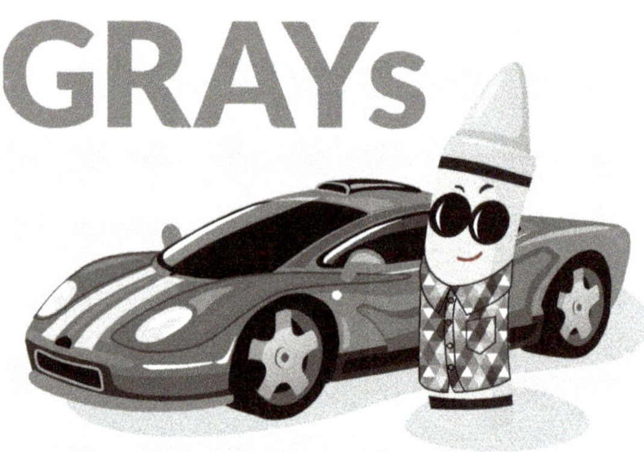

GRAYs are neutral. They represent balance—the balance between White and Black. Because of this it can soften the harsh contrast in a Black and White setting. Adding Gray (sometimes referred to as grayscale) will give more depth to an otherwise high-contrast design.

You can find this color in brand logos like **Apple, Swarovski, Wikipedia,** and more. Apple also uses Gray or Silver tones in many of its product designs.

➕ POTENTIALLY POSITIVE EFFECTS

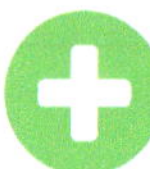

Neutrality and Versatility: Gray is a neutral color that can serve as a versatile backdrop for other elements. It complements a wide range of colors, creating a sense of balance.

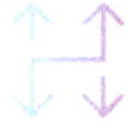

Timelessness and Classic Appeal: Gray's timeless quality can portray a sense of elegance and classic appeal with understated sophistication.

Minimalism and Simplicity: Gray can be minimalistic, creating a clean, simple, and sleek aesthetic. It can allow other elements to take center stage.

Professionalism and Seriousness: Gray can convey a sense of professionalism, formality, and seriousness often used in corporate settings or industries.

➖ POTENTIALLY NEGATIVE EFFECTS

Lack of Vibrancy: Gray, being a neutral color, may lack vibrancy or dynamism on its own. Too much Gray can appear dull or monotonous.

Emotionless or Cold Impression: Gray can create a sense of detachment or aloofness, giving the feeling of being emotionless or cold.

Lack of Distinctiveness: Gray is a common color, but it may lack distinctiveness or struggle to stand out independently. Relying solely on Gray may not stand out in the market place.

ℹ SOME CULTURAL DIFFERENCES

In some cultures, Gray is associated with modesty and humility. In other cultures, gray can be associated with maturity, wisdom, and experience. Gray also represents sobriety, formality, and seriousness.

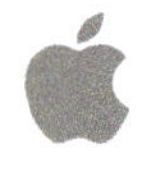
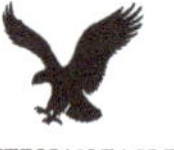
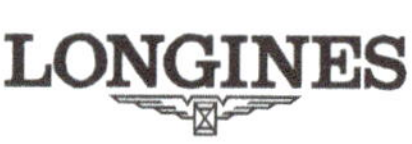
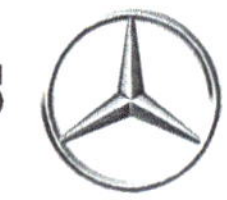
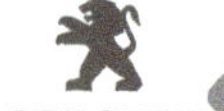
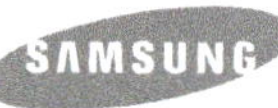
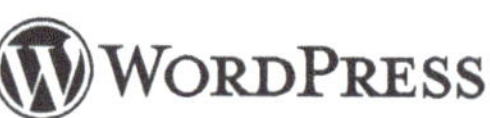

BROWNs

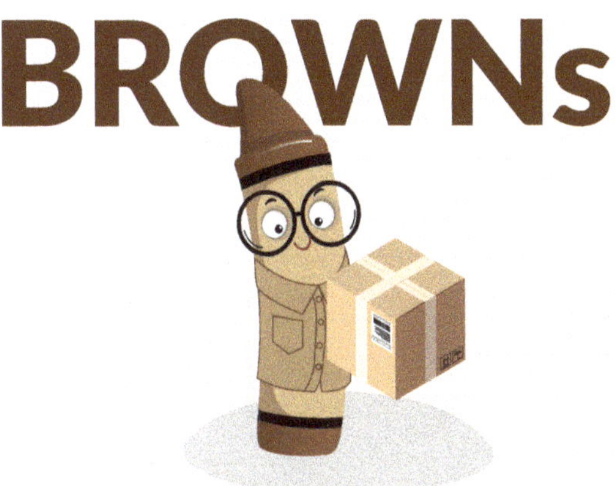

BROWNs are the colors of the earth, wood, and stones. Therefore, they represent comfort, security, and a down to earth nature. You will find a lot of companies that promote natural products use this color in their branding strategy. One of the most famous brands that use the color Brown is **UPS**. In fact, their motto is "Trust Brown."

Since Brown is also the color of chocolate, **Hershey's, M&M,** and other chocolatiers use it in their logos and branding.

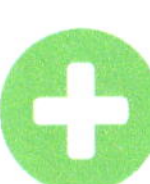
Warmth and Earthiness: Brown is often associated with warmth, earthiness, and nature, which create a cozy and inviting atmosphere.

Reliability and Durability: Brown can convey a sense of reliability, durability, and strength. It is often associated with sturdy materials like wood and leather.

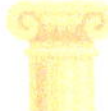
Simplicity and Timelessness: Brown has a simplicity and timelessness that can evoke a sense of classic appeal, creating a vintage or nostalgic atmosphere and a sense of tradition.

Warmth and Comfort: With a warm and comforting quality, Brown can create a sense of familiarity and reassurance. It can be nurturing, evoking feelings of reliability and trust.

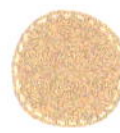
Dullness or Muddiness: Brown, a muted color, may be perceived as dull, muddy, or lackluster.

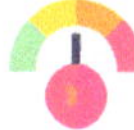
Limited Versatility: Brown may be limited in versatility compared to other colors, which could make it challenging to pair with certain colors or create a striking contrast.

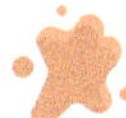
Association with Dirt or Unpleasantness: In certain contexts, Brown may be associated with dirt, decay, or unpleasantness, creating negative connotations.

Brown has universally similar effects, so it's not surprising that some cultures consider it to represent their cultural heritage and traditions and stand for rootedness and groundedness.

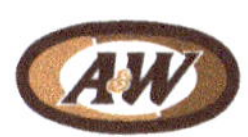
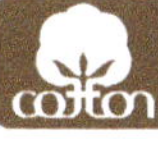
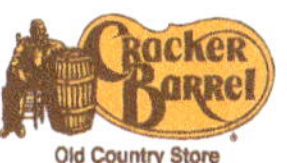
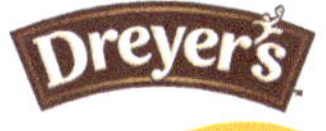
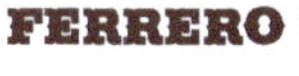
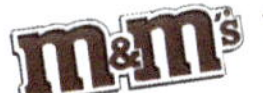
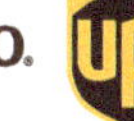

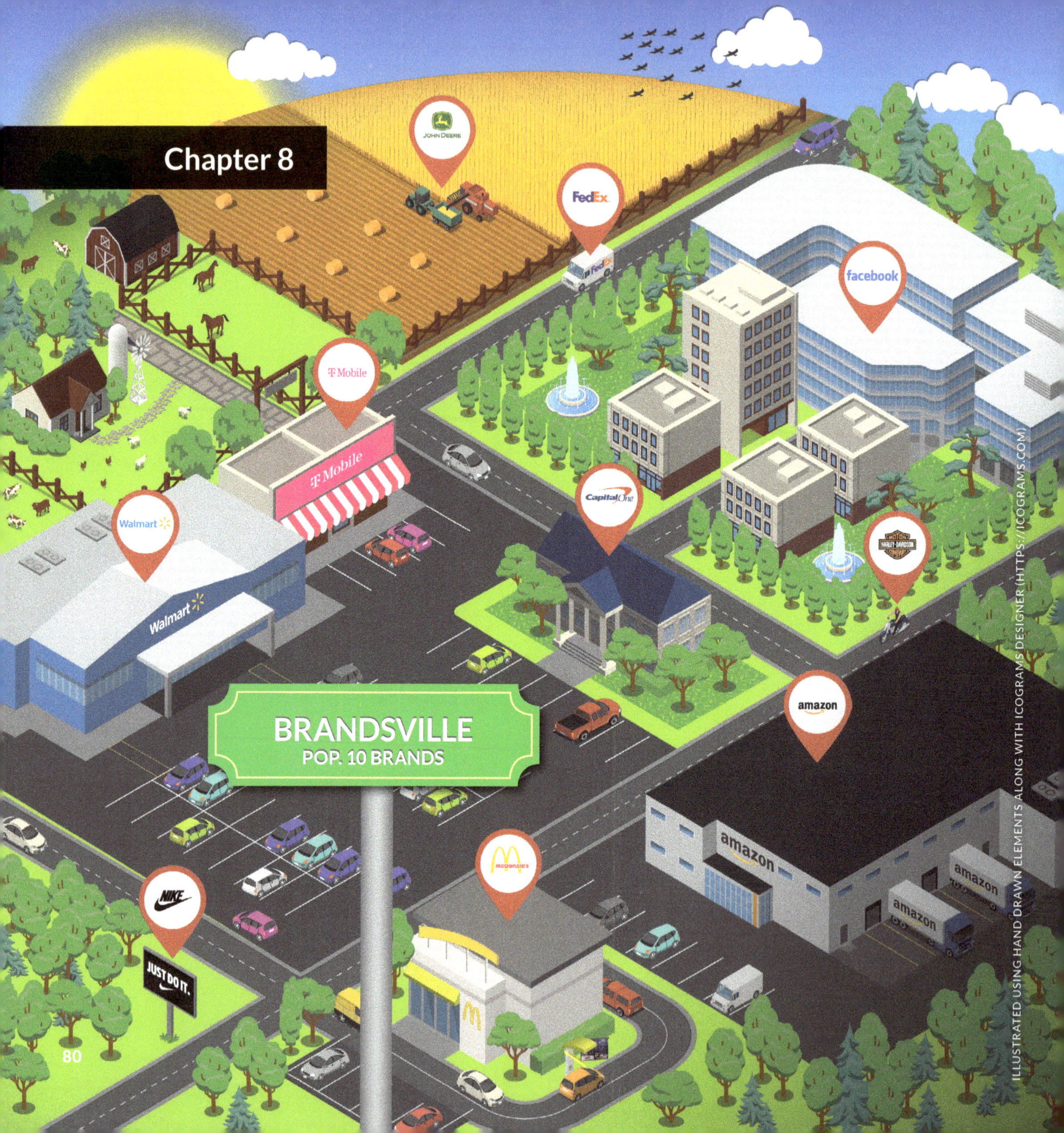

Chapter 8
JOHN DEERE
FedEx
facebook
T Mobile
Walmart
Capital One
HARLEY-DAVIDSON
amazon
BRANDSVILLE
POP. 10 BRANDS
NIKE
JUST DO IT.
McDonald's
amazon
80
ILLUSTRATED USING HAND DRAWN ELEMENTS ALONG WITH ICOGRAMS DESIGNER (HTTPS://ICOGRAMS.COM)

A Tour of Brandsville

In this chapter, we will explore why ten of the most popular brands across several industries chose their brand colors. I'll share a little about their brand identity story—how they got to where they are today. And I'm hoping you can glean some wisdom from their journey. The ten brands we'll discuss alphabetically are Amazon, CapitalOne, Facebook, FedEx, Harley Davidson, John Deere, McDonald's, Nike, T-Mobile, and Walmart.

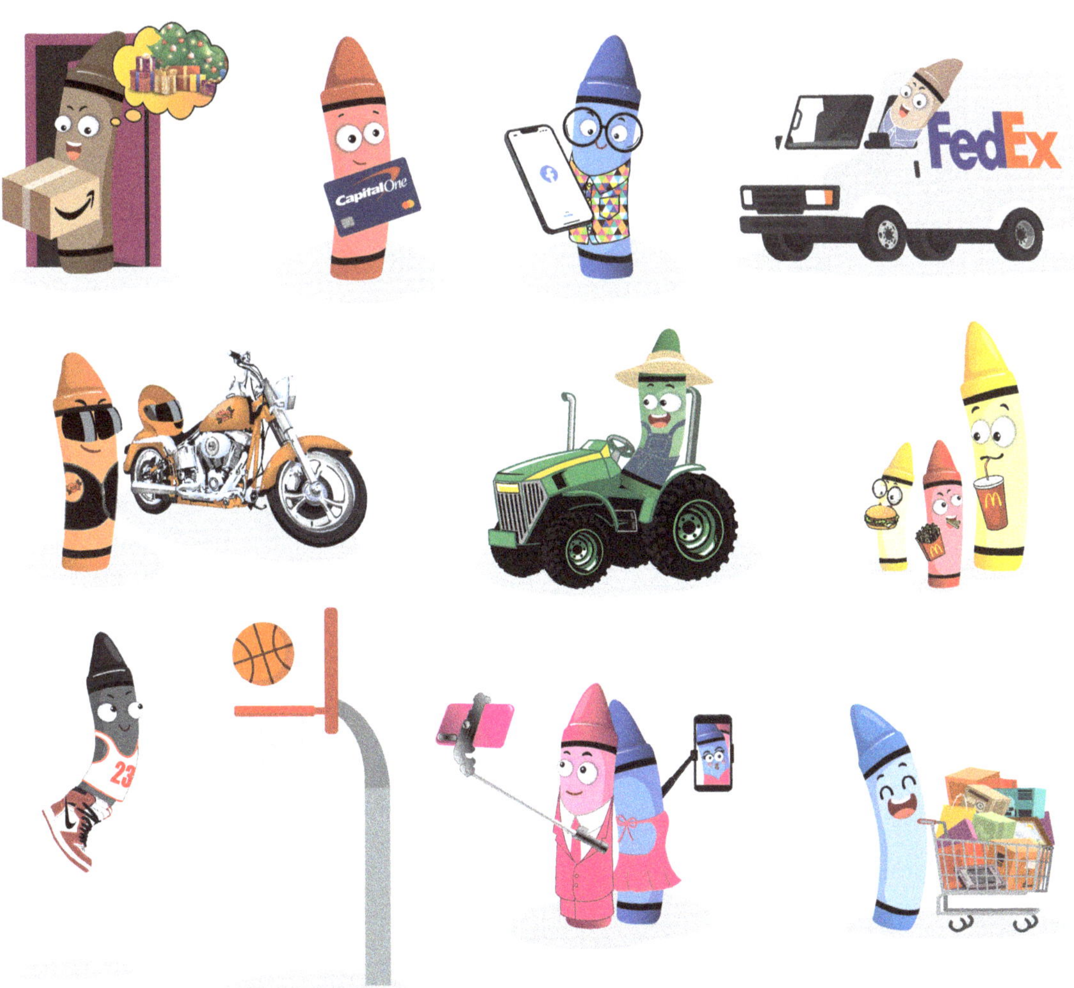

OLEKSANDR - STOCK.ADOBE.COM

Amazon

Amazon's bold, contrasting use of Black and Orange in its branding has made its logo distinct and recognizable worldwide. Other companies use this color combination to attract customer attention, but none are as effective as Amazon. This powerful combo has led to Amazon's strong brand recognition.

The Black font, a color often associated with *professionalism* and *sophistication*, makes the text easy to read and reproduce. Whether I see their logo on my phone, an ad, a package, a delivery truck, or anywhere else, I instantly recognize their brand, and it immediately gives an impression of *trustworthiness* and *credibility* for the company. This is further highlighted by the streak of Orange, a *vibrant* arrow pointing from A to Z, which resembles a smile, indicating that they make their customers *happy*. I know that opening my door to an Amazon package always makes me happy. It feels like Christmas!

Orange represents *friendliness* and adds a flair of *vibrancy* and *energy*, portraying the company's dedication to offering maximum variety, purchasing ease, budget-friendly savings, and customer *happiness* and *satisfaction*. It's precisely the combination that customers, myself included, want in an online shopping experience: professionalism, *reliability*, and *care*.

Together, the Black and Orange create a sharp *contrast* which makes the logo visually *appealing* and also *versatile* in use, able to be used across many mediums including digital and print. This creates unity and consistency in their brand, and overall has led to Amazon being universally recognizable even in the crowded e-commerce marketplace.

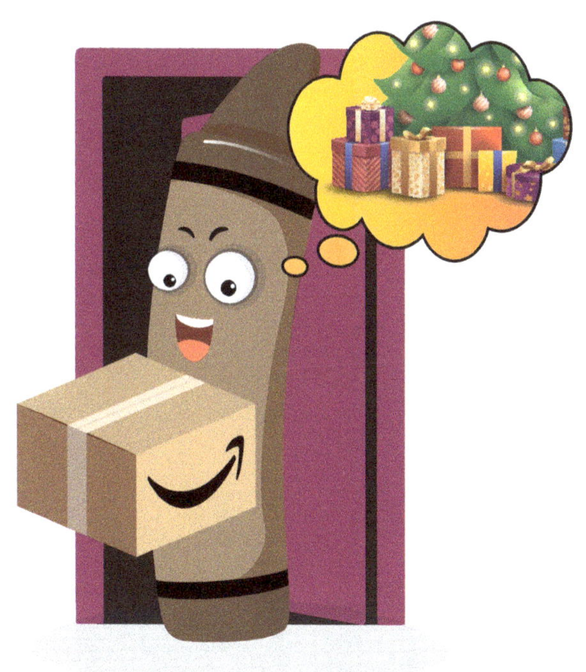

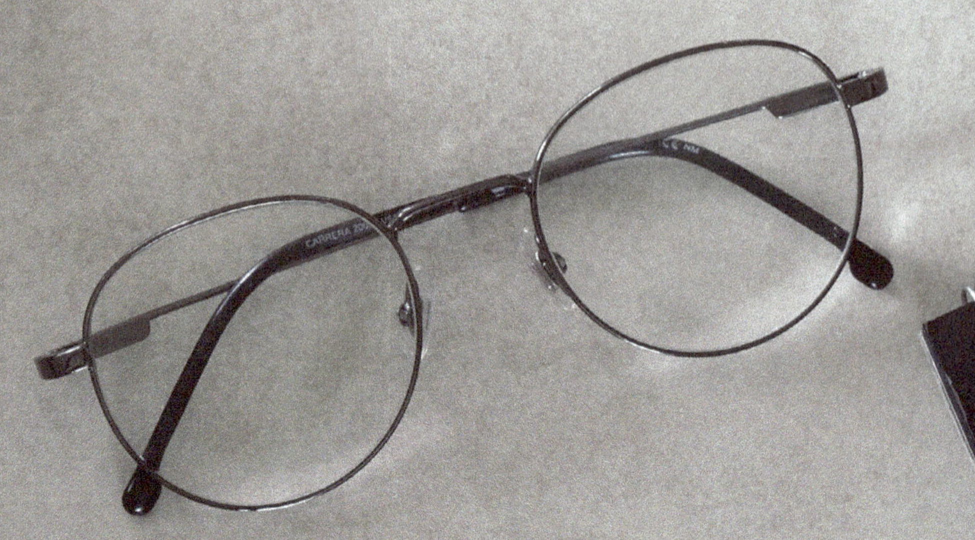

ИГОРЬ ГОЛОВНЁВ · STOCK.ADOBE.COM

CapitalOne

Since its founding in 1988, CapitalOne's visual identity has been defined by its Red, White, and Blue logo. As with any successful business, a strong brand identity is vital. CapitalOne has achieved its universal recognition as a leader in the banking and financial services sector due, in part, to its consistent use of this powerful visual brand.

Even the specific color shades were carefully chosen, and its color palette has become iconic over the decades. Blue is a color suggestive of *trustworthiness, coolness, and intelligence.* These characteristics are especially important when used in association with caring for customers' money and financial future, giving a sense of *stability* and *security.* It's not unusual for many companies in the financial sector to incorporate Blue into their branding for this reason—these are all qualities that I, for one, desire in a bank and financial institution.

CapitalOne also capitalizes on this solid link to the financial world to show customers they are a *credible* company aligned with industry expertise and expectations. White is a symbol of *cleanliness, purity, and clarity,* while Red is one of *power, aggression, confidence,* and *energy* and imparts a sense of urgency. The Red, used in the swoosh symbol, resembles a check mark (or boomerang) and gives the impression of *growth* and *consistency.* It's a color attractive to customers looking for an *innovative* and *cutting-edge* company that will fulfill their promises with *integrity, swiftness, and confidence.*

Together, the logo conveys a *professional, knowledgeable,* and *empowered* identity. Both Blue and Red are universally understood and recognizable as colors, making them widely *accessible* and an effective marketing tool across cultures and demographics. Since the color palette has been used consistently since its founding, CapitalOne is clearly established in its brand image. Therefore the message communicated to its customers is *clear* and *reliable.*

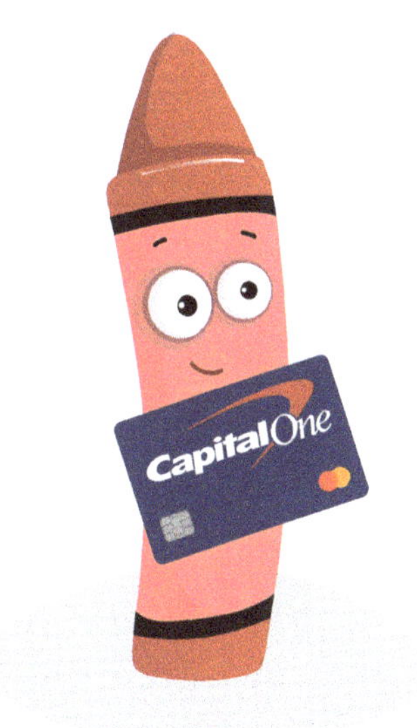

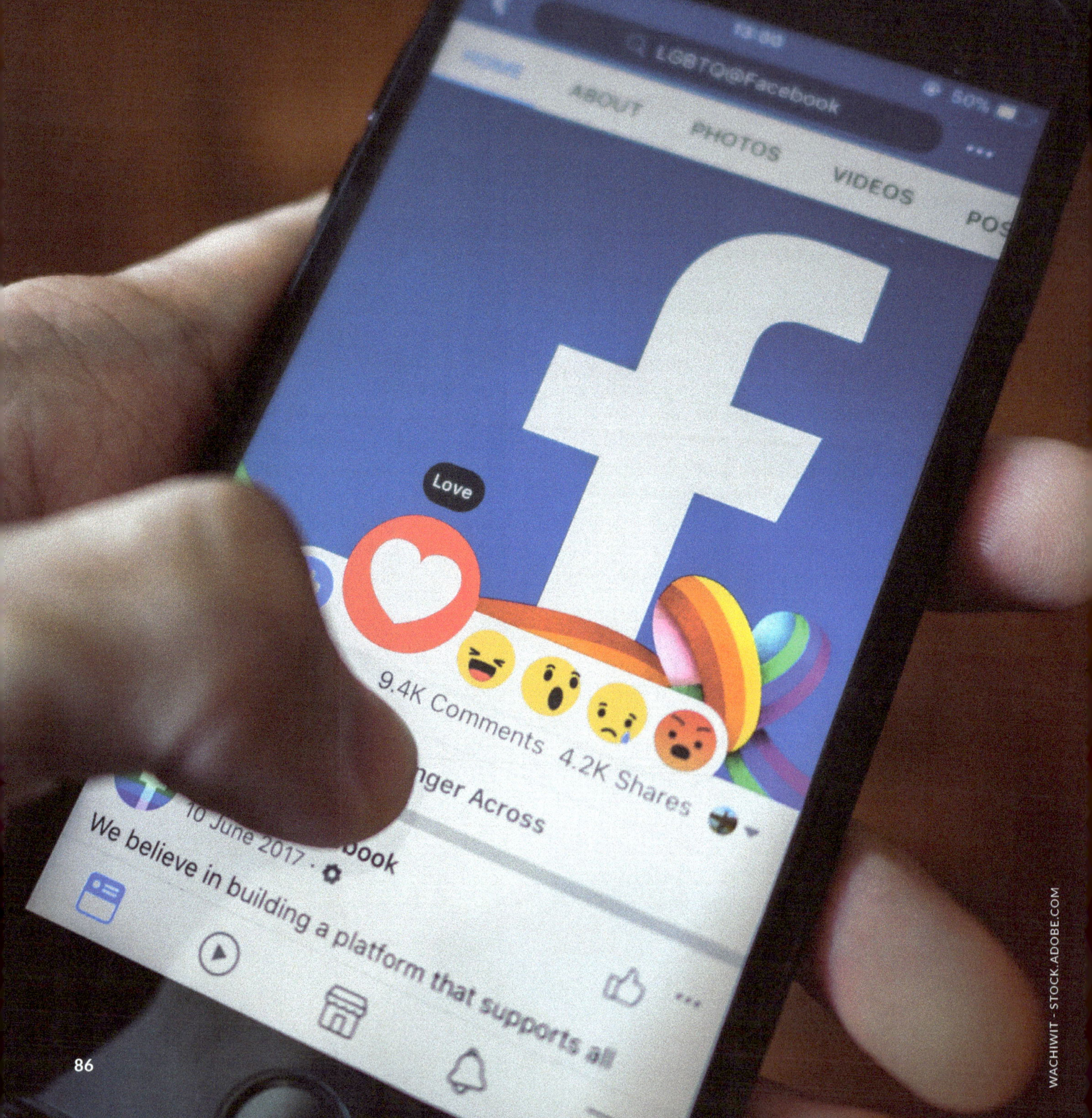

WACHIWIT · STOCK.ADOBE.COM

Facebook

There is one color that comes to mind when you think of Facebook, and that's Blue. Among its core values as a company are community, openness, and connection, and Mark Zuckerberg was wise for many reasons to choose Blue as the company's primary brand color. Initially, Zuckerberg chose Blue for one reason: he is Red-Green colorblind.

However, in the years since its founding, his color choice has proven far more impactful for the company's success for other reasons. While Facebook's success can't solely be attributed to its brand color, the unification of the visual brand with its overall user experience, functionality, and value have no doubt helped to shape the company's image with customers and users across the globe.

As you'll remember from previous entries, Blue is a color associated with *trust, reliability, safety,* and *security,* reinforcing the company's mission to "make the world more open and connected." The bright, vibrant Blue has come to be known as Facebook Blue. It is now identifiable anywhere—app, website, ad, or billboard. This universal recognition and the psychology of the color choice inspire feelings of reliability, *confidence* in the platform, and *connection.*

The secondary color in Facebook's logo is an Off-White, giving a feeling of simple *luxury.* Together, the Blue and White make a *clean* and *modern* image that keeps the focus on the content, ideas, and available space for connection.

Facebook desires to inspire loyalty and create a safe space for emotional connection with and between users. It has done so in a *unique* and *global* capacity with its simple design and use of color making it *accessible* and *understandable* across cultures and language barriers.

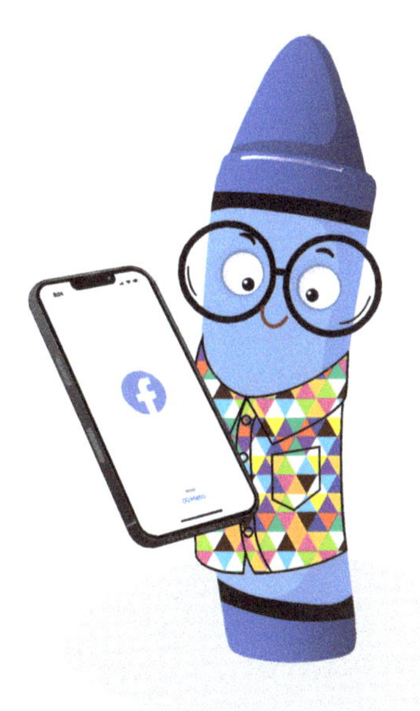

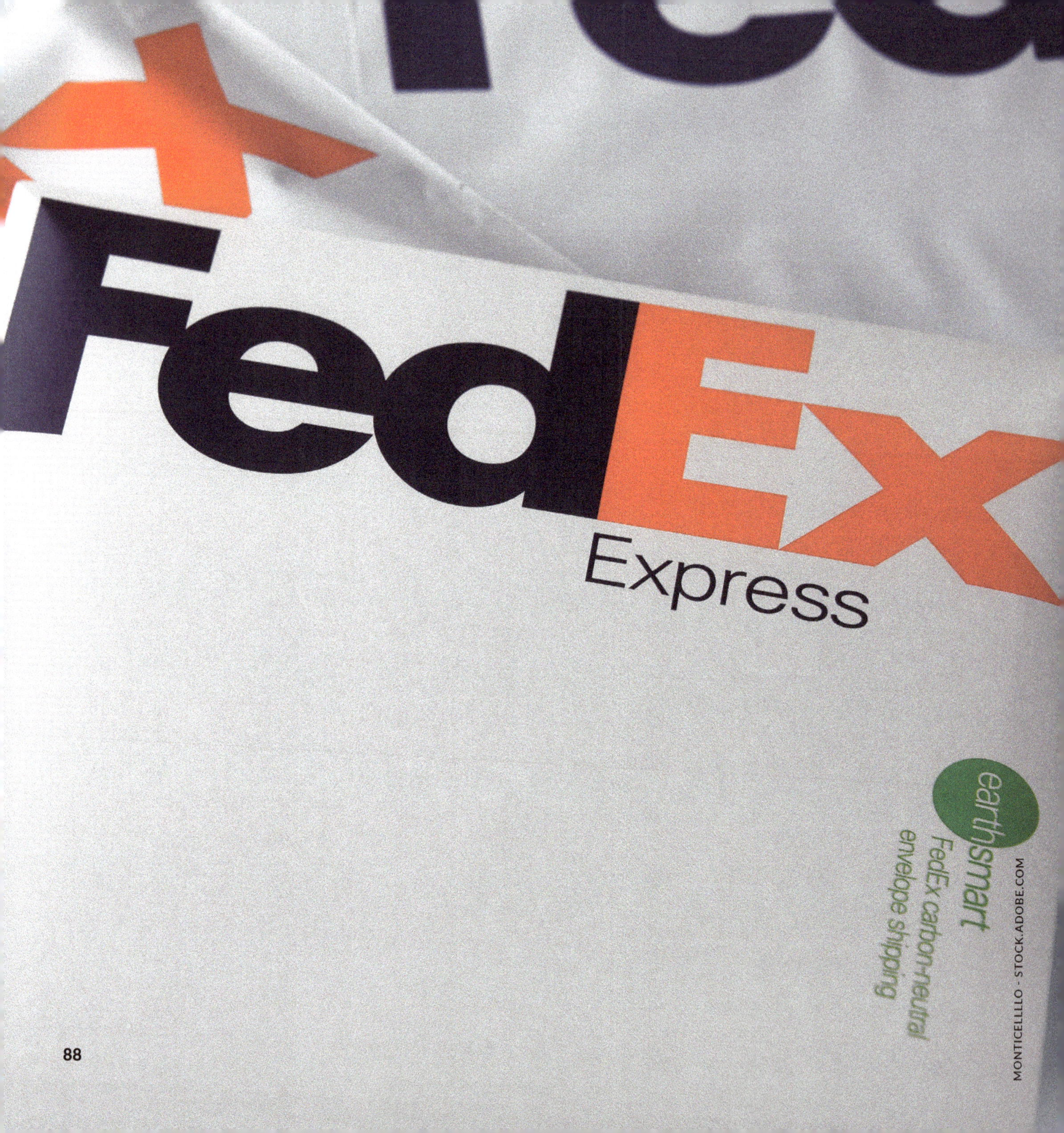

FedEx
FedEx
Express
earthsmart
FedEx carbon-neutral
envelope shipping
MONTICELLLO · STOCK.ADOBE.COM

FedEx

FedEx's award-winning logo, though initially an accident, has become known as one of the most effective ever created. Originally designed in 1994 by London Leader with Landor Associates, they realized partway through design that the negative space between the capital E and the lower-case x formed an arrow, which subtly speaks to the company's promise to deliver goods from point A to point B reliably, swiftly, and accurately.

In addition, the brand colors Purple and Orange form a compelling combination. The two colors boldly contrast each other, making the vibrant logo instantly *memorable* and *recognizable*. This differentiates it from almost all of FedEx's competitors, who often use Blue or Red in their branding.

This *distinct* color scheme allows FedEx to stand out and not only makes the logo visible and readable across different mediums and distances and to those with color blindness, but also suggests the company is *innovative* and *forward-thinking* compared to competitors. Purple, which has long been a symbol of *royalty, luxury,* and *quality*, shows FedEx's commitment to *professionalism, trustworthiness,* and *expertise.* After all, what customer wouldn't want to be treated like royalty? I find reassurance in knowing my packages will be handled with care and expedience.

Orange, representative of *friendliness* and *enthusiasm,* similarly reflects FedEx's

value of exceptional customer service. Both Purple and Orange are also *culturally neutral,* making the logo *globally appealing,* which is vital for a multinational brand.

Overall, the effective use of Purple and Orange in FedEx's brand identity has contributed to its strong recognition, *differentiation,* and association with *reliability* and exceptional customer service. The color combination stands out, ensures visibility, and creates a memorable impression in the minds of consumers.

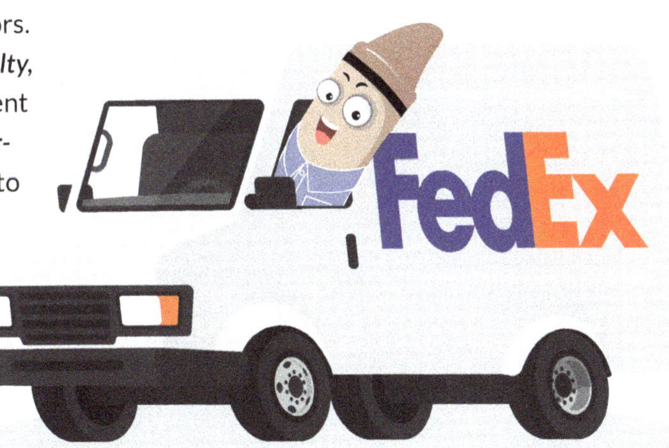

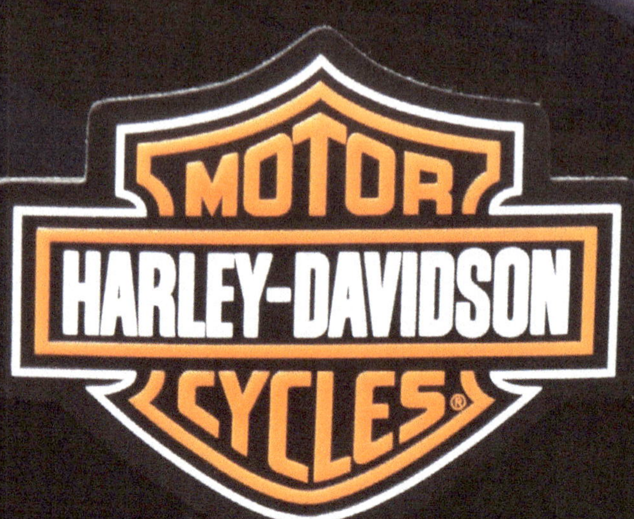

INSIDEPORTUGAL - STOCK.ADOBE.COM

Harley-Davidson

Harley Davidson, founded more than 100 years ago, is an iconic brand known not only for its motorcycles and culturally for its spirit of adventure but also for its powerful logo design. The logo has evolved since the company's original founding. Unlike other vehicle companies, each dealership can have its own version, some adding different wings or embellishments to the original design.

However, even with the updates and dealership variations, the logo has remained largely loyal to the bar and shield format, and no matter what dealership you visit, you will always see the emblem of the shield and bar, the Black, White and Orange colors, and the strong, stylized sans-serif font.

This basic logo continuity across all dealerships reinforces the strength in its symbolism, the bar and shield representing the brand's *strength* and *durability*. Eagle wings are also commonly used in celebratory logos and by many dealerships, and reinforces Harley-Davidson as an all-American company.

Black, Orange, and White as primary colors are high-contrast, bold, and *powerful* colors that exude Harley Davidson's strong, *adventurous*, *rugged*, and *rebellious* image, which their customers and target audience can strongly identify with their own values of *freedom* and *individuality*. Black is a color that conveys *authority*, power, and *dominance*, and Orange is associated with *energy*, *optimism*, and a spirit of adventure.

Harley Davidson uses White to contrast with the Black and Orange for a modern and *sophisticated* facet to the brand. Black and Orange create a strong contrast, and the dark and bright color contrast creates a strong visual presence, captivating image, and overall an emotional *connection* to its target audience by appealing to their core values and the rich heritage of motorcycle culture in America. Have you ever noticed that some Harley Davidson motorcycle owners start to look similar to their motorcycle?

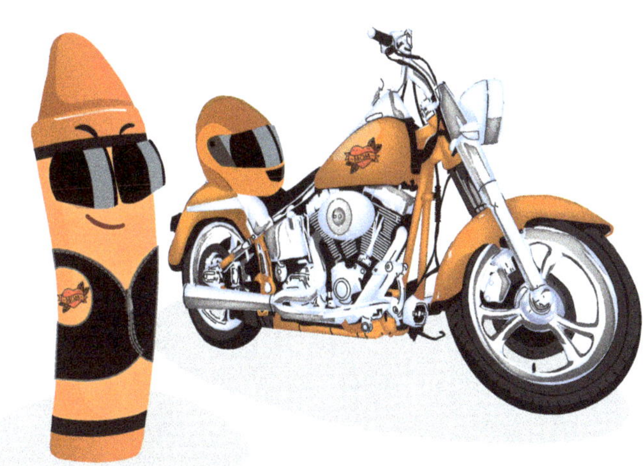

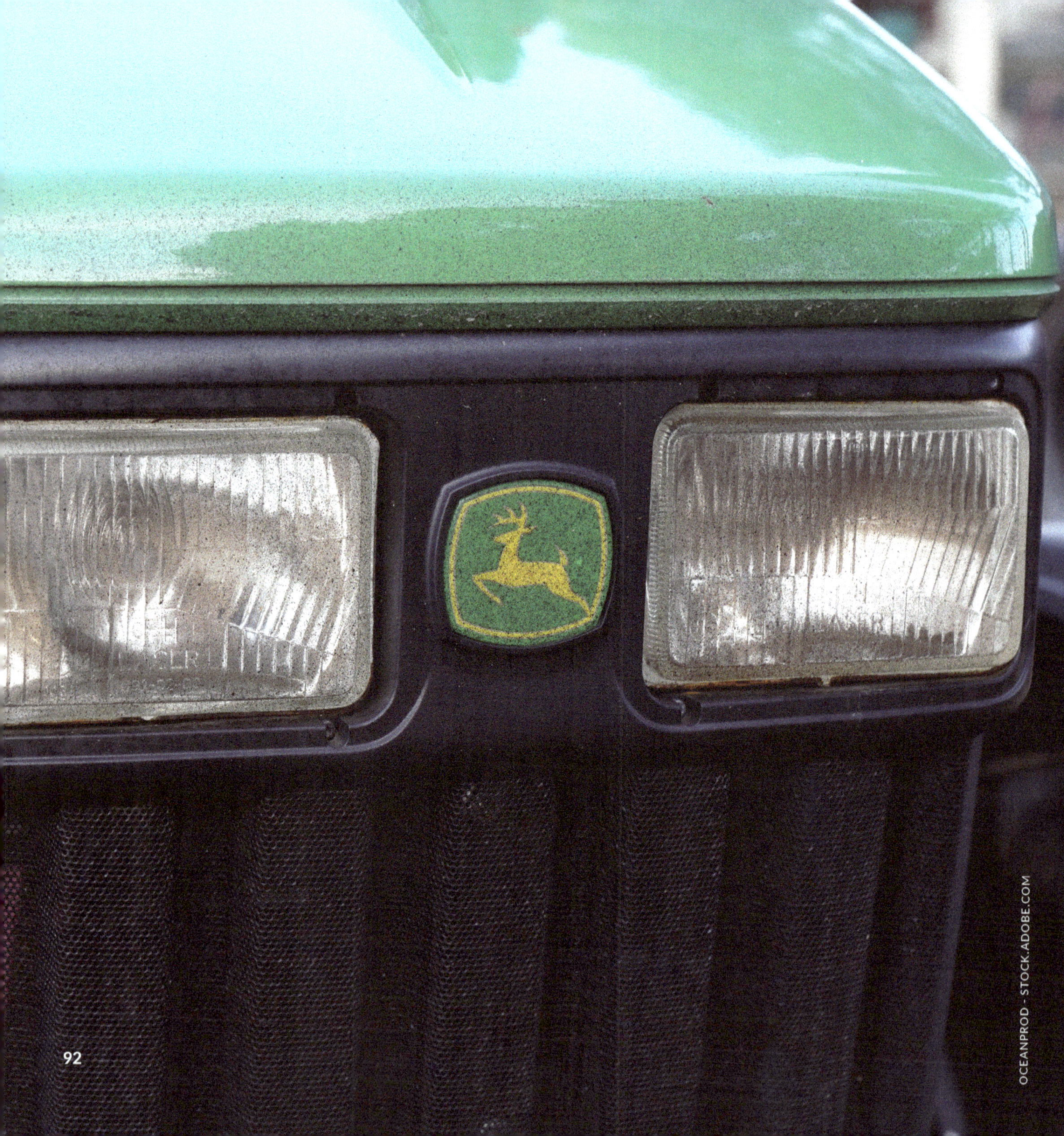

OCEANPROD - STOCK.ADOBE.COM

John Deere

John Deere has been using a variation of the galloping deer since the 1870s and has been incorporating the colors of Green and Yellow into its brand since the 1880s. Throughout the decades, the logo has evolved to reflect the mission and values of the brand, and it wasn't until the year 2000 that the logo we all recognize today was established.

Until 2000, the logo itself had been Black and White, though the brand already had a solid and reliable visual identity in the iconic Green and Yellow colors. These colors were originally used to paint the company's first wagons in the 1800s and have been used consistently ever since for equipment, marketing campaigns, and product lines.

For an agricultural company, the choice of the color Green is obvious. Green is everywhere associated with *nature*, *fertility*, and *growth*. Yellow, a bright color symbolic of *vibrancy* and *optimism*, demonstrates *hope* for the future.The combination of these two colors draws a clear correlation between John Deere's equipment and nature, growth, and *life*. The color palette has *warmth* and *friendliness*, reflecting the company's mission to provide innovative tools for helping its customers succeed, grow, and thrive.

To complement John Deere's use of color is the image of the deer itself, designed to be gracefully leaping forward to symbolize the company's *strength*, *stability*, *perseverance*, and *dedication* to *hard work* and *innovation*. The deer also further highlights the company's *connection to nature*. Between its consistent use of its brand image for over 100 years, and its strategic use of color to highlight the company values and promises, John Deere has successfully established itself as an iconic and universally recognized brand, one that customers can be assured of its quality before even making the purchase.

Whenever I see a Green tractor on the road or in a field, I know that it is a John Deere.

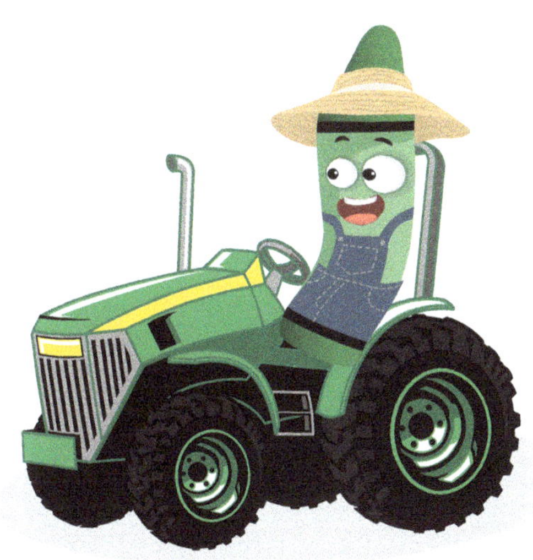

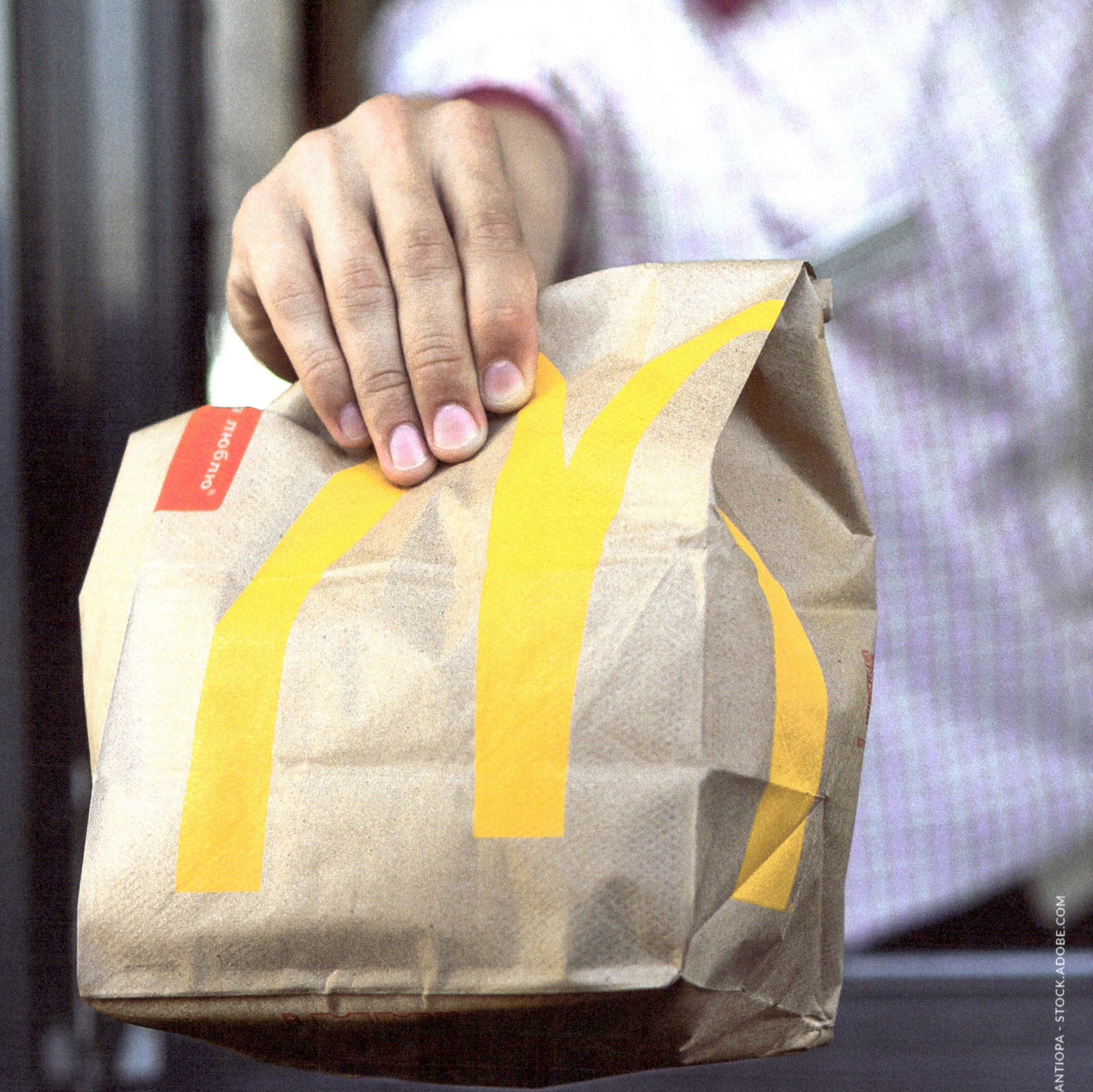

GARGANTIOPA - STOCK.ADOBE.COM

McDonald's

Arguably the most recognizable brand in the world, since its founding in 1955, McDonald's has been highly intentional in its visual branding and representation. Picture a McDonald's, and if you're like me, you'll immediately think of those giant golden arches.

Memorable not just because of the simple "M" for McDonald's but because of that bright, welcoming shade of Yellow. It's a stimulating color, one that promises a *high-energy* and *positive experience*. The Red backdrop similarly conveys *excitement, passion,* and *action,* creating a sense of *urgency* that contributes to a rapid turnover of customers. This is the fast food experience they're promising, after all.

The combination of these two primary colors is powerful. Not only has the unique pairing made the brand instantly *recognizable,* but the two contrasting colors ensure that the logo will always be clearly *visible* by customers and will stand out on any background, whether it be on an ad or a billboard.

The two colors also evoke *more excitement* than they would on their own, creating a sense of impending *enjoyment* and *nostalgia,* evoking feelings of childhood *innocence* through the almost childish colors that bring up those *warm, fuzzy feelings of comfort*—and desire for comfort food. We don't necessarily walk into a McDonald's with the expectation of fine-dining, but one of *indulgence* and *familiarity,* a feeling that will have us too thinking, "I'm lovin' it." The psychology of the two colors goes even deeper, however, with studies showing that Red and Yellow can be used to *stimulate appetite* and *increase cravings* and *hunger.* Even reading this case study and analyzing the logo has me craving some McDonald's fries. Red and Yellow are also considered lucky colors in many cultures, making the brand not only instantly recognizable but also *universally favorable.* It's interesting to note, however, that in Europe, McDonald's has begun to introduce Dark Green instead of Red in order to portray an image that is more eco-friendly.

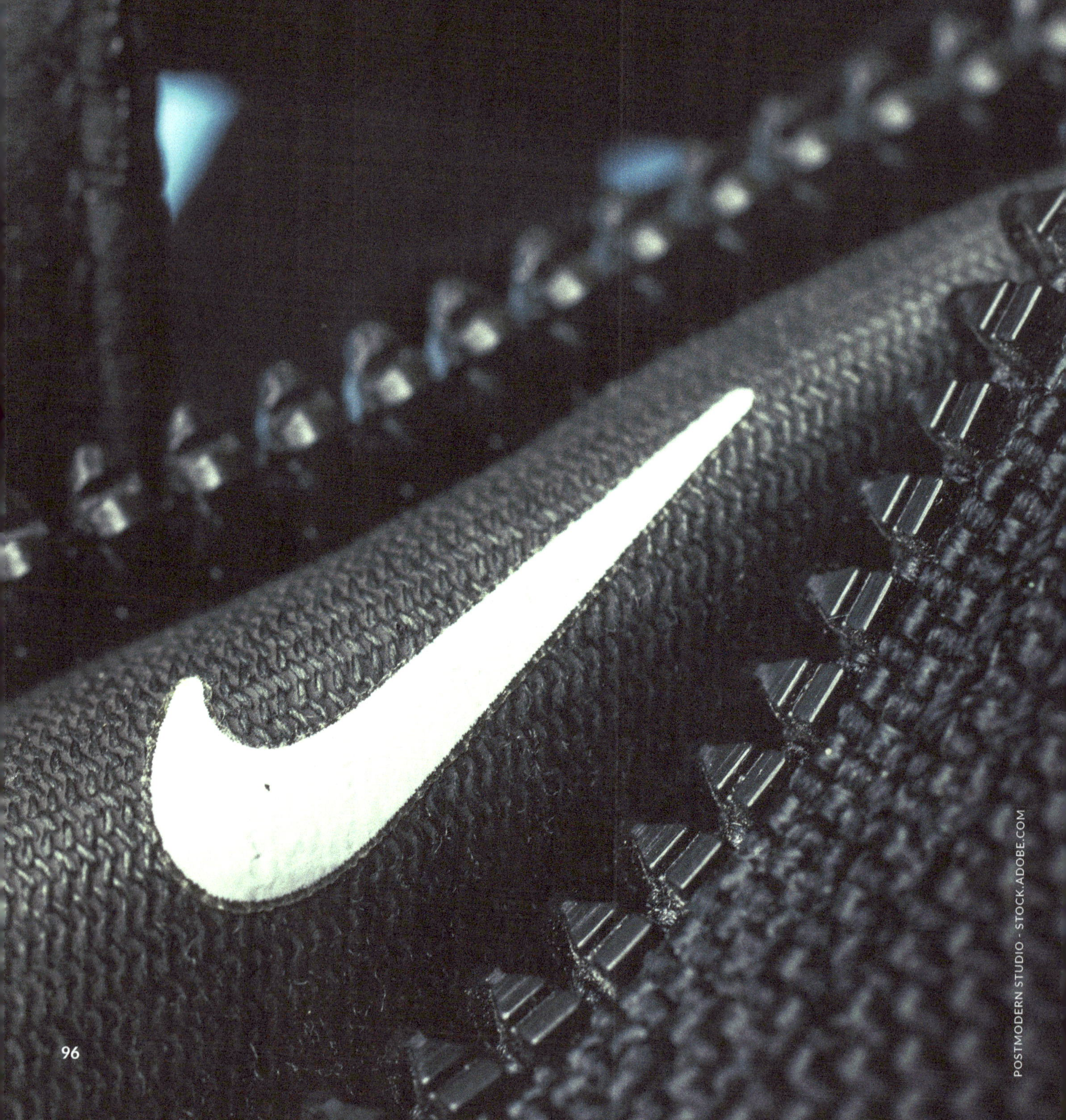

POSTMODERN STUDIO · STOCK.ADOBE.COM

Nike

The Nike swoosh logo was created in 1971 by Carolyn Davidson, who had been commissioned by Phil Knight, the co-founder of Nike, to create a design that was drastically different from their competitor, Adidas. It took Davidson 17 and a half hours to design the logo. Originally called the "strip," the simple and elegant logo represented the idea of movement that Nike wanted to be associated with.

For the first several years, Nike used the swoosh in the colors of Red and White—Red to represent *power*, *speed*, and *passion*, and White to show *loyalty* and *transparency*. The logo colors were later changed to Black and White, and this was more effective for the company overall for several reasons.

First, this was more effective for its *contrast* and *simplicity*. Nothing contrasts quite like Black and White, and high contrast ensures that a viewer's attention will immediately be caught as well as be easily viewable and legible no matter the medium. Similarly, Black and White are *versatile* and can be used easily in print or digitally, on any kind of product, and in marketing campaigns.

Second, Black and White are *classic, universally appealing* colors that evoke a sense of *timelessness*, *elegance*, and *sophistication*, further establishing Nike as a global brand. While Black and White have a *classic appeal*, they also reflect the company's relevance in *modern* times, as the colors also reflect *clarity* and *cleanliness*, positioning Nike as *innovative* and *cutting-edge*. The *minimalism* and *simplicity* also allow viewers and customers to focus on the actual product and athlete endorsement themselves. Finally, Black and White also improve the *legibility* for individuals with either visual impairments or color blindness.

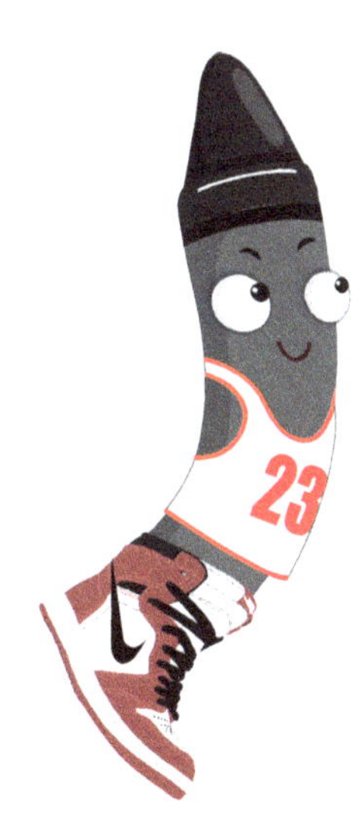

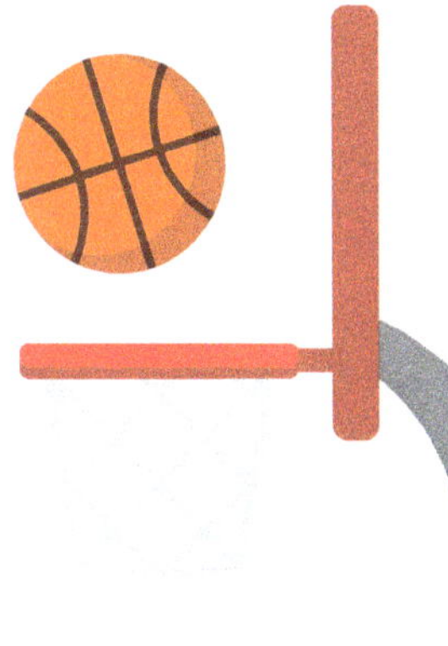

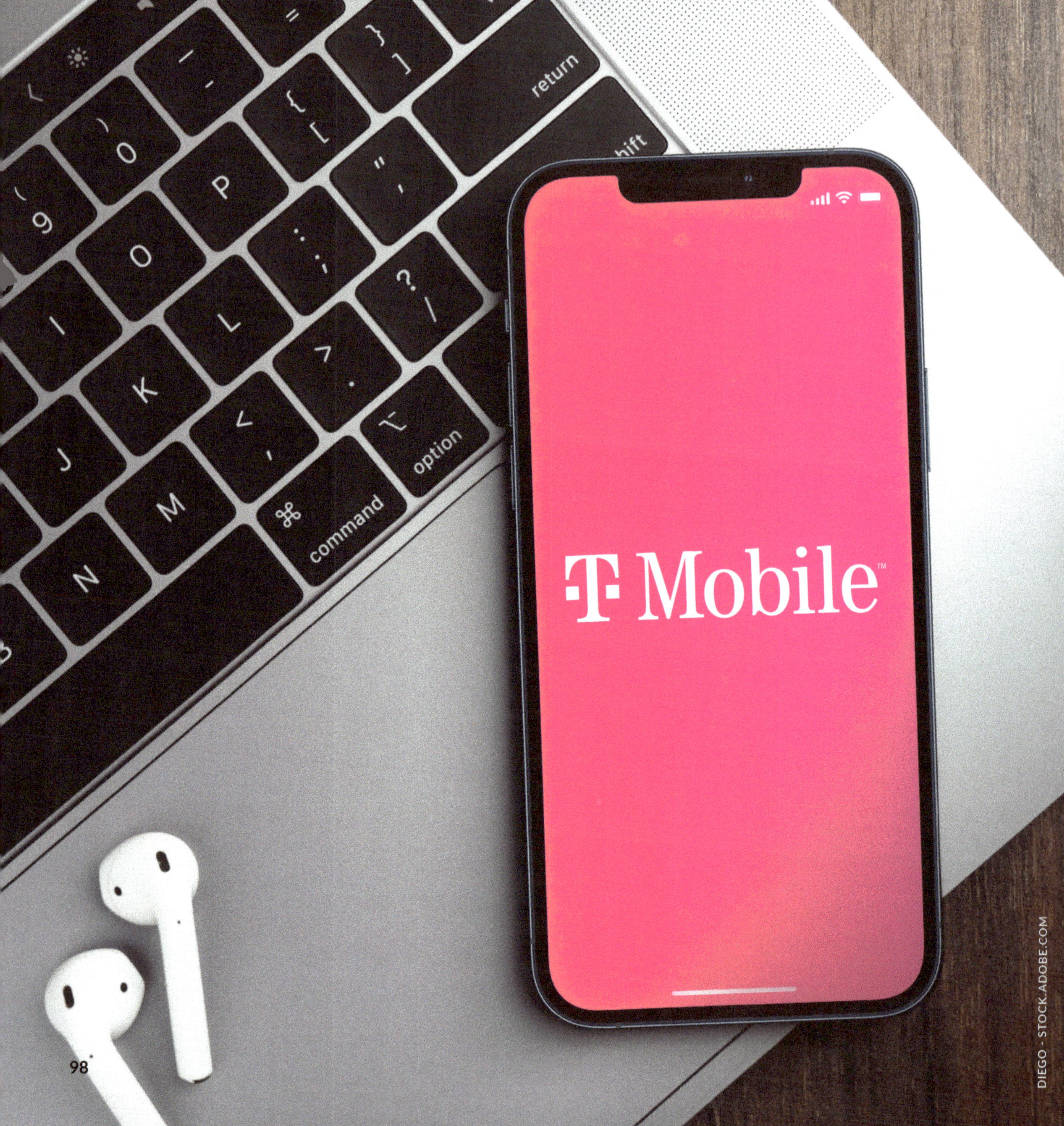

DIEGO - STOCK.ADOBE.COM

T-Mobile

Sleek and simple, the logo is instantly recognizable and clearly demonstrates the company's specialization. T-Mobile, a group of companies within the mobile communications field, is owned by German telecommunications company Deutsche Telekom and operate GSM net-works in Europe and the United States.

The letter "T" in the design thus stands for "Telekom." T-Mobile has about 109 million subscribers and is the 4th largest cellular operator worldwide. Probably the most vital aspect of T-Mobile's brand design has been its use of the color Magenta, which has allowed it to stand apart from all other companies in the telecommunications industry.

Magenta, which is a bright shade of Pink, represents *joy* and *passion*; against its White background, it immediately catches viewers' eyes and creates a *bold* and *energetic* presence that simultaneously conveys *innovation* and *dynamism*, further establishing T-Mobile as a disruptive and progressive competitor in the marketplace.

T-Mobile has very strong brand recognition as a result, and its simplicity and consistent use in logo, branding materials, ads, retail spaces, and more, have firmly established the brand in the mind's of consumers, as well as Magenta as the official color of the company. The brightness, contrast, and *simplicity* also make the design highly readable and visible and create a sense of *modernism* that makes it appealing to

younger and more tech-savvy demographics. As a result, T-Mobile has achieved global recognition and appeal.

This is one brand that uses a variation of Pink that appeals to all demographics. I for one, appreciate companies that push the boundaries on stereotyping with color.

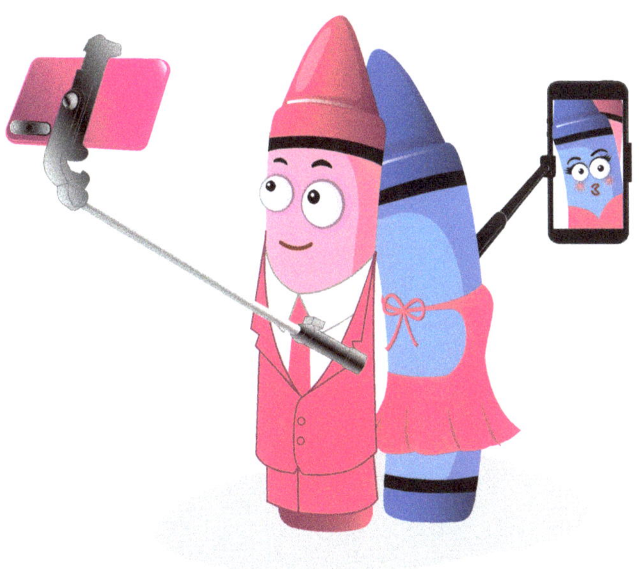

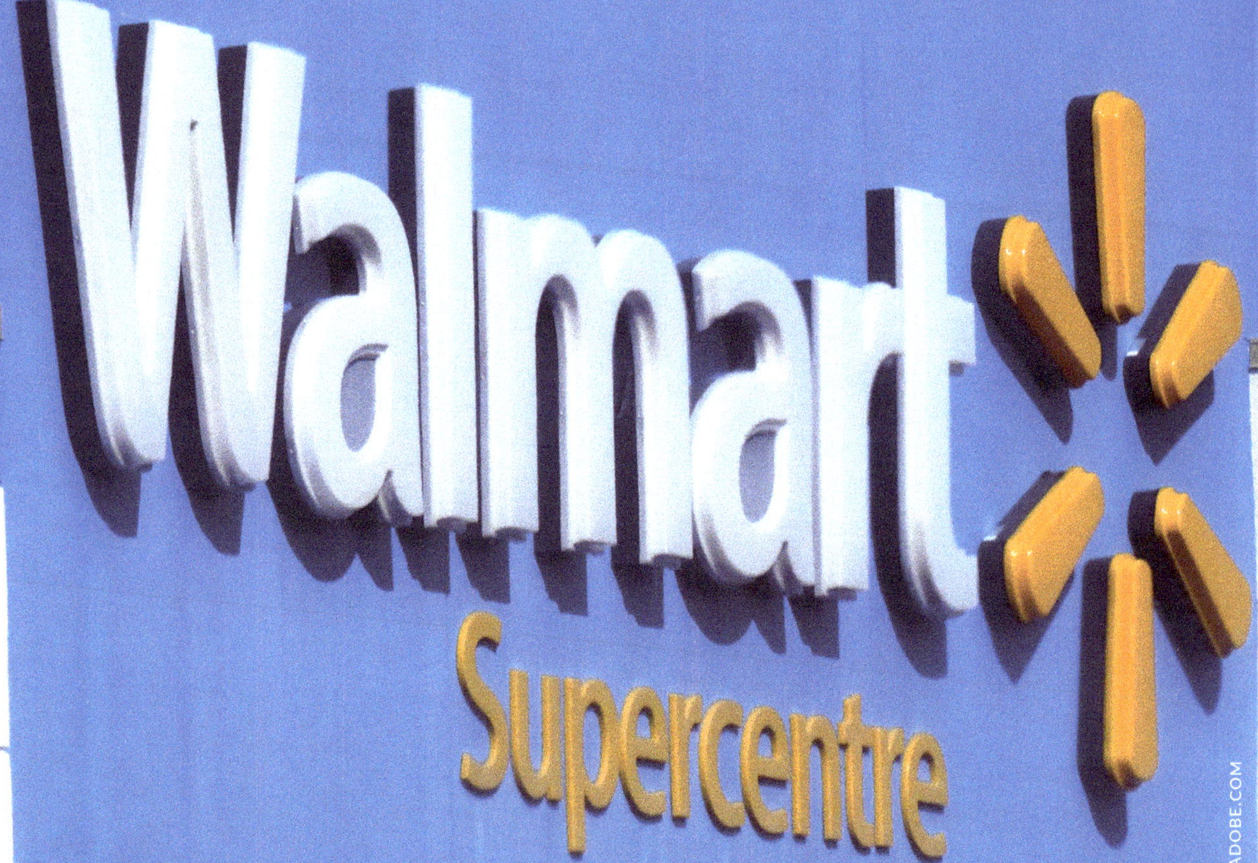

OASISAMUEL - STOCK.ADOBE.COM

Walmart

Walmart's Blue and Yellow logo is among the most iconic anywhere, an accolade befitting the world's largest retailer, with annual sales exceeding $600 billion. As Walmart has grown from Sam Walton's single store in 1950 to today's 10 thousand stores across 24 countries, the brand and logo have kept pace with changing shoppers.

A major redesign in 2008 produced the current Walmart logo, which moved for the first time from a sans serif font in all caps to a capitalized W only. It is followed by what the company calls a warm, sun-like "spark," an homage to Sam Walton's original inspiration spark to empower customers to, as he said, "save and have a better life." That focus lives on, and I know I can always trust Walmart to provide the best value.

Lippincott, Walmart's branding agency, devised the spark to energize the previous logo featuring a generic Black star, used from 1992 to 2008. That star had, in turn, replaced the hyphen that united "WAL" and "MART." The pre-2008 version was dark Blue, representing *trust* and *dependability*, then became medium Blue to appear more *youthful*. The golden spark, evoking feelings of *friendliness* and *warmth*, was conceived with six spokes, or "sparklets," representing Walmart's six core values: a focus on customers, respect, integrity, great associates, service and excellence. Putting Blue and Yellow together—a genius decision—yielded a high-contrast logo that boosts Walmart's visibility and branding everywhere.

The current logo is meant to appeal to today's changing customers, whose preferences tend toward more eco-conscious and high-end goods. For Walmart, its customers are the boss. Walmart knows their expectations are going up, and it is transforming its goods and services to serve them ever better.

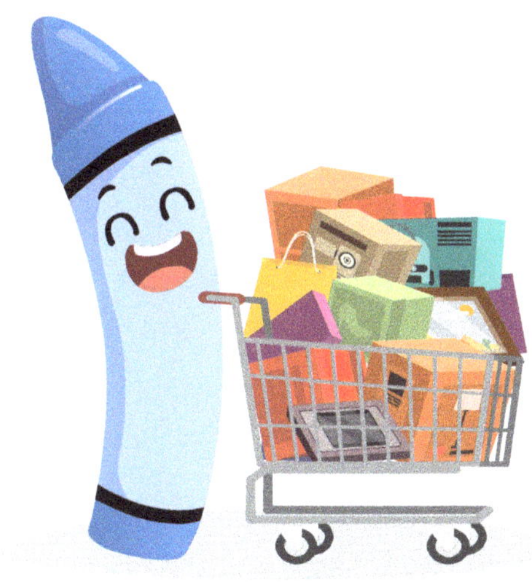

Chapter 9

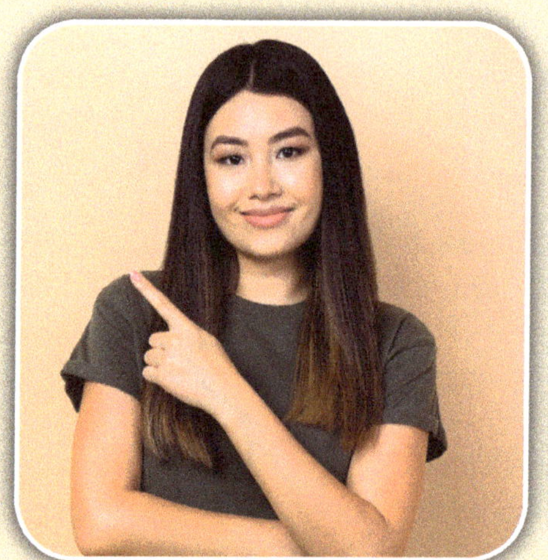

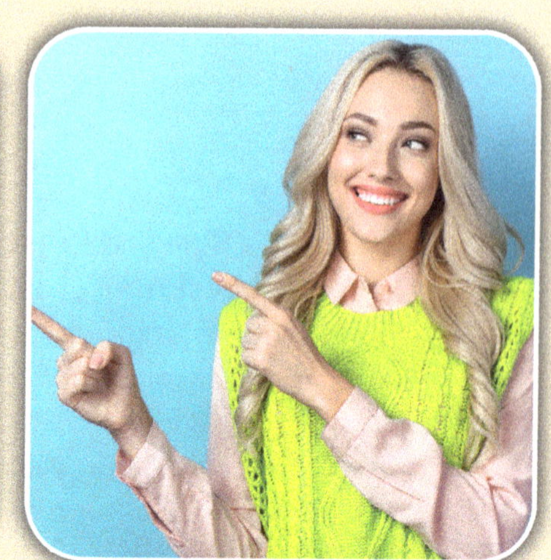

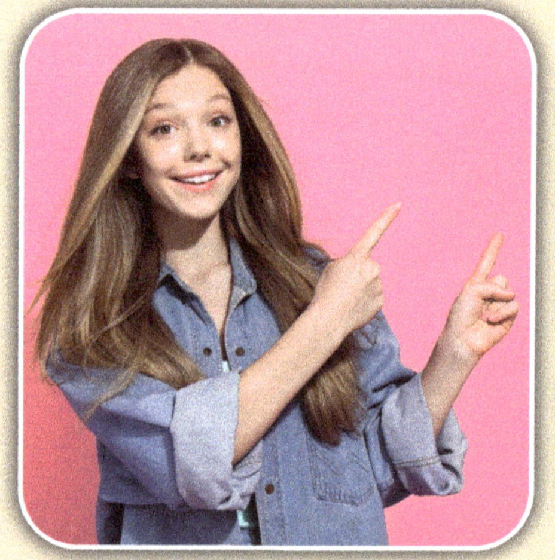

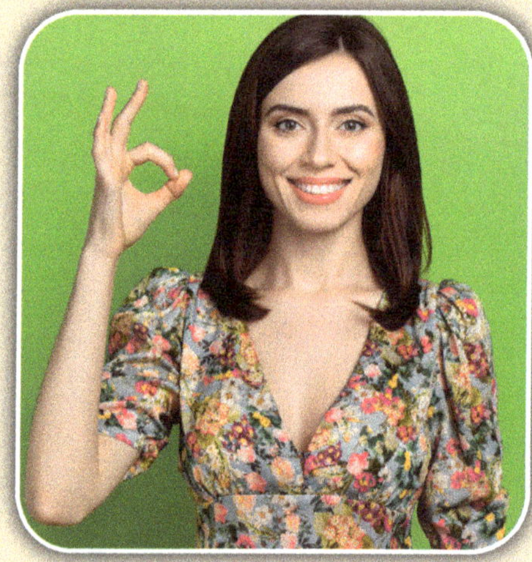

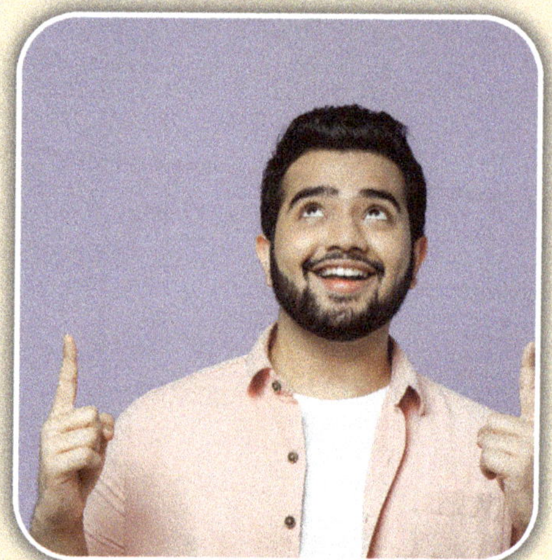

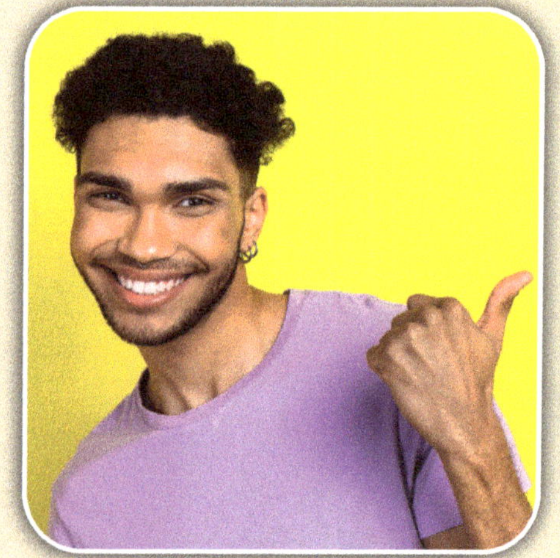

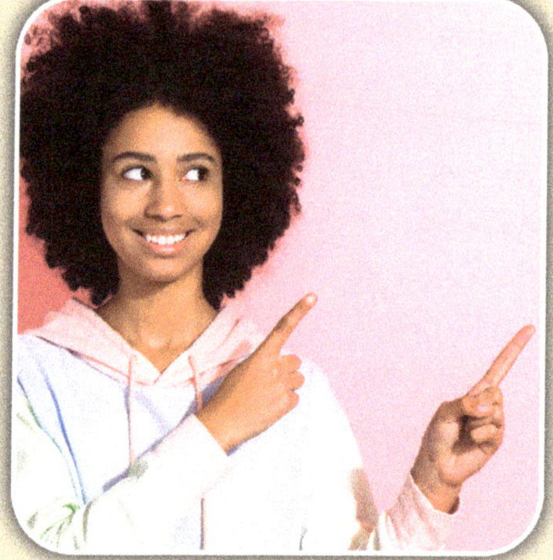

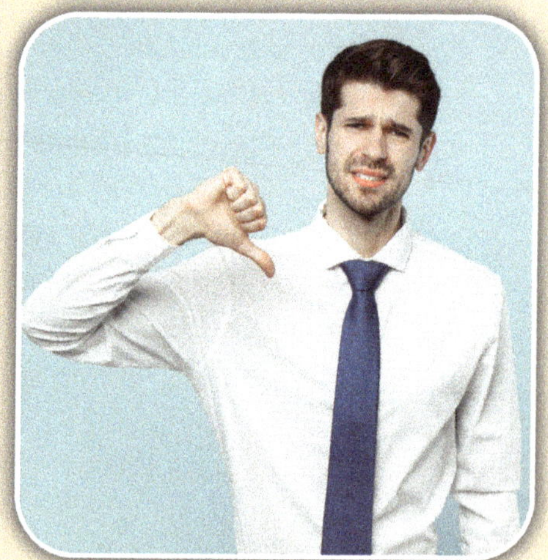

Brand Personality Matters

Even though there are a lot of variables involved and some debate with color theory and color psychology, there are still facts that can't be ignored. According to a study "Impact of Color on Marketing" conducted by Satyendra Singh, an associate professor at the University of Winnipeg in Winnipeg, Canada, it takes around 90 seconds for a consumer to create an opinion about a product. Out of those 90 seconds, 60-90 percent of that interaction is based on the color of the product or the brand.

With businesses increasing their online presence by the droves, and new businesses opening up left and right, color psychology is one of the things that business owners, managers, entrepreneurs, and others should use to help stand out and outshine the competitors.

Whether you're into landscaping, retail, hospitality, B2B, or any other industry, your success heavily depends on the colors that you choose to use and the impression that you choose to give. Your brand's personality is everything!

Where to Use Color

The proper question should be: Where shouldn't we use color. Colors are ubiquitous, just like oxygen. You use them in your logos, websites, social media channels, marketing, branding, promotional products, signage, and everywhere else.

Color and Consumer Purchases

According to color psychology, different colors have different effects on the moods and behaviors of consumers. They can either calm them down or increase their anxiety. Not only that, but the color of the product also says a lot about the personality of the consumers. There's a reason why people buy a specific color of car.

The colors you choose for yourself say a lot about you and the image you are trying to project. This means the clothes you wear, the car you buy, the paint you use in your house, and everything in between makes a statement about how you want people to look at you.

The needs of the audience are never the same. You might like one color at one time in life and another color at another time. It all depends on various factors like age, gender, culture, environment, and more.

Your consumers' personalities play a crucial role in color psychology. For example, a person might want to buy a White car, not because they want to look modern and clean, but because the climate of the area where they live is hot. People who live in hot climates usually

What's Your Brand Personality?

Brands tend to fall into one or more of five core traits with one dominating according to the paper, *"Dimensions of Brand Personality"*

by Jennifer Aaker

Sincerity

Down-to-earth

Family-oriented · Small-town

Honest

Sincere · Real

Wholesome

Original

Cheerful

Sentimental · Friendly

Excitement

Daring

Trendy · Exciting

Spirited

Cool · Young

Imaginative

Unique

Up-to-date

Independent · Contemporary

Competence

Reliable

Hard-working · Secure

Intelligent

Technical · Corporate

Successful

Leader · Confident

Sophistication

Upper-class

Glamorous · Good looking

Charming

Feminine · Smooth

Ruggedness

Outdoorsy

Masculine · Western

Tough

Rugged

SOURCE: HTTPS://WWW.GSB.STANFORD.EDU/FACULTY-RESEARCH/WORKING-PAPERS/DIMENSIONS-BRAND-PERSONALITY. DESIGN BY JANIE OWEN-BUGH

prefer cars, house exterior paint, etc., in light colors instead of dark.

The Importance of Color in Marketing

So, what have we learned so far?

We've learned that if you want to establish your brand as something different than everyone else and leave your competitors behind, then you want to use everything that you can to create a difference. You want to stand apart from every other brand in the market and one of the ways that you can do that is by using the best colors in your branding and marketing.

The right color can set you apart, and although there isn't per se a wrong color, you can run the risk of blending into the crowd or driving away your target audience. In a sea of brands, the color strategies in your marketing efforts can enable your audience to see you in a new light. They can help you create a brand personality that you want and help your customers perceive you as you want to be perceived.

In her paper "Dimensions of Brand Personality," Jennifer Aaker, a psychologist and Stanford professor writes that after conducting studies, she discovered five core dimensions that play a role in a brand's personality (see infographic on opposite page). She points out that brands can fall under more than one trait but one

usually dominates. Do you know which one your brand is under?

After reading this book, I hope you will be able to choose the best colors for your brand, logo, website, or more. Remember that what you choose, can enhance your brand perception or make it just another face in the crowd. Let's choose something memorable.

In Professor Singh's study, "Impact of Color on Marketing," the researchers found that more than 90% of the judgment that consumers made about a specific product were based on the color. Also, another study called "The Interactive Effects of Colors and Products on Perceptions of Brand Logo Appropriateness," by Paul A. Bottomley and John R. Doyle of the Cardiff Business School in the UK, observed that whether a color works for a brand or not depends on whether the color is deemed appropriate for that particular brand. So, in other words your branding strategy should take into consideration whether your brand colors are appropriate for your specific industry or niche.

Colors have been proven to drive the brand's personality, and consumers consider the brand's color before purchasing the product or service. This was revealed in the study "Exciting Red and Competent Blue" by Lauren I. Labrecque and George R Milne in the Journal of the Academy of Marketing Science. They say

Tone

Is my brand
playful or serious?
Why?

Value

Is my brand
luxurious or affordable?
Why?

Time

Is my brand
modern or classic?
Why?

Age

Is my brand
youthful or mature?
Why?

Energy

Is my brand
loud or subdued?
Why?

Gender

Is my brand traditionally
masculine or feminine?
Why?

that color influences likability and familiarity. Which seems logical to me. Why else would you want to buy a Harley Davidson, if you didn't get the *rugged*, *free*, and *cool* feelings associated with Orange and Black? Why would you buy a Ferrari if it doesn't give you a sense of *freedom* (Yellow), *luxury* (Black and White), and *adventure* (Red and Green)?

Further studies show that when we go out to buy something or when we shop online, our brains look for recognizable brands. That is why colors matter so much in branding strategies. They are one of the first things that people notice when interacting with a brand.

What Colors Work Best for You?

How can you find the one or more colors that work best for your brand? It all depends on your brand and its personality. You know that customers don't buy a product, they go for the personality attached to that product or brand. On the opposite page, you will find a worksheet with questions you can ask yourself to determine your brand's personality.

Your answers will give you an idea of what your brand personality could be. You can use that to see what color(s) works best for you.

Where to Start?

Choose several colors and test them out. There is no such thing as a single color for a specific place. Just because so many high tech companies are using sliver in their logo doesn't mean that you have to do the same. Just because most of the CTAs (call-to-action) that you've looked at are Red doesn't mean that you have to follow the trend.

Check different colors by placing them in your CTAs. Then, do A/B testing (a marketing technique that compares two versions of a web page or application to see which performs better, also known as split testing) or show it to a few loyal customers, your employees, family, and friends, and get their feedback. Don't just leave the color choice up to your designer.

As a designer myself, I typically know more about colors and their effects than most of my clients. But there are a few who have done their homework and know about as much as I do. It makes it fun to work with them. I get to share my ideas, listen to their ideas, and come up with something truly magnificent.

What I'm trying to say here is that no matter who you work with, make sure that the colors you use are not just meant to look good. They are also meant to attract consumers and convert them to customers or clients.

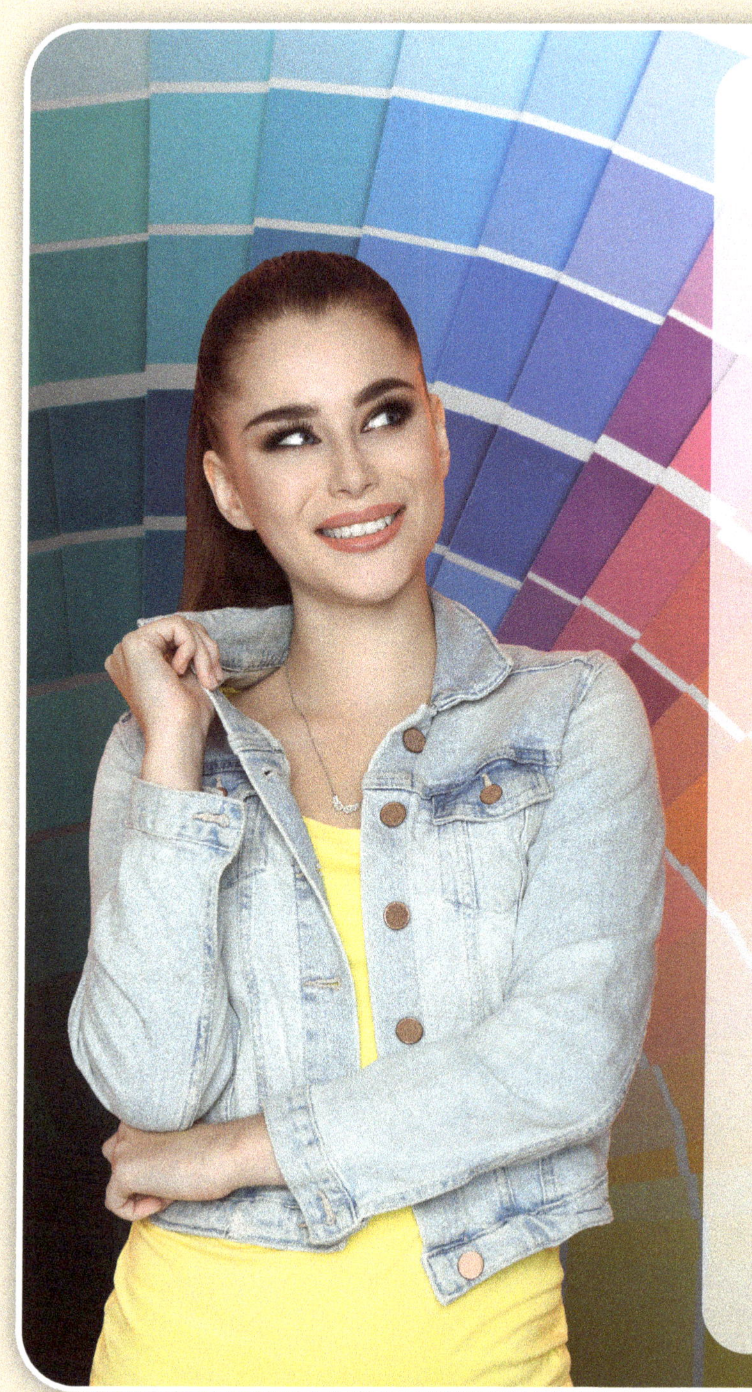

You did it!

Now that you're
Color-Confident,
you're ready
to go out and

Color Your
Brand &
More!

Avoid Color Overload.

Going overboard with color usage is always a temptation. I struggle with that myself, because I love color so much. In today's DIY mentality, it's easy to get carried away. But, too many colors tends to confuse customers. Try keeping your color palette to a minimum of two to five colors, max. Sometimes, corporations and even smaller companies have lots of products or services and those companies will tend to have more colors in their color palette. Some colors are used particularly for certain products or services they are associated with. If that's you, I say, "go for it."

From Color-Challenged to Color-Confident

The world is a colorful place, and if we just think about it, a lot can be done with those colors. Let go of the "what if I make a mistake" mindset and analyze your brand, your audience, and your products and services.

Now, you may already have a brand with products/services, and you might not be in a position to make any big changes. There are many things you can do, small enough things that won't make a whole lot of difference to your brand style guide but will make a big bang in how customers perceive your brand.

There might be a time when you will feel the need to rebrand. Maybe you didn't know about color psychology at the time of your original branding, but now you do. If you want your brand to have a personality that your target audience can connect with and relate with, then consider making a change.

No matter what you decide to do, color is your decision to make. All I've done here is give you the tools to give you confidence to make the best color decision for your brand. I can't wait to see what you come up with.

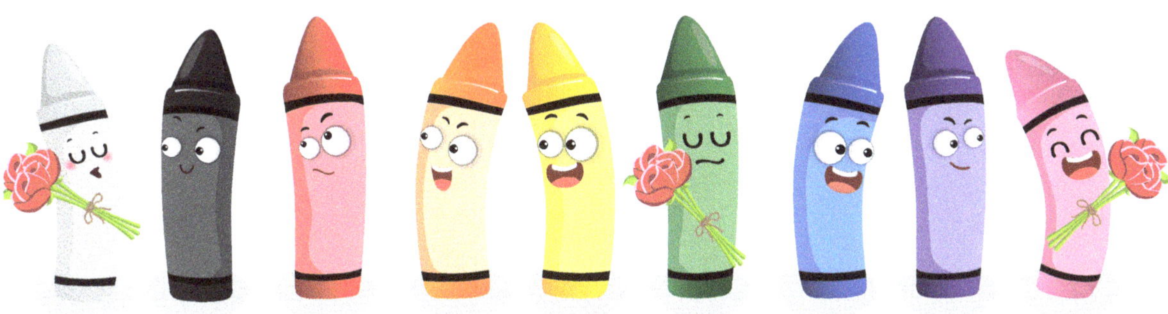

Summing it Up

In Chapter 6, we talked about how colors can effect our mood and our buying decisions based on several studies done on the subject. In Chapter 7, we dove head first into 11 colors and how they effect our brands, both negatively and positively, as well as culturally. Then, in Chapter 8, we took a tour of Brandsville and explored why 10 popular brands may have chosen their colors. And, finally, we wrap up the entire book in Chapter 9 with some suggestions and takeaways to help you get started on your color journey.

What Have You Learned So Far?

Let's test your knowledge about color effects and the psychology behind it. Answer the questions below, then compare them to the answer key on page 116 to find out how you did.

1. Colors can have both positive and negative effects on consumers, but there are some factors that could come into play like culture. Name 3 other factors:

   • _______________________________________

   • _______________________________________

   • _______________________________________

2. People can develop a preference or a dislike for a color based on emotional experiences they've had with that particular color in their past.
   True or False? _____________

3. According to Faber Birren's study, using ____________ colors like Green or Blue causes people to underestimate the passage of time while using ____________ colors like Red and Yellow makes them overestimate the passage of time.

4. The isolation effect is when something stands out like a sore thumb and will likely soon be forgotten.
   True or False? ____________

5. What is the most popular brand color?

   ____

6. The following is a table of effect symbols. Please fill out the table according to the headings of each column. Under the Effects column **name at least two effects** associated with the symbol; then, tell whether it is

a **positive or negative** effect under the Pos/Neg? column; and lastly, **name one or more colors** that can have that effect.

Symbol	Effects	Pos/Neg?	Color(s)

7. Of all the brands in Brandsville, which one's brand color(s) were chosen because the CEO is color blind? ___________________________

8. Which brand in Brandsville probably chose their color(s) to encourage fast turnover, satisfied customers? ___________________________

9. According to Professor Singh's study, it takes around 90 seconds for a consumer to create an opinion about a product. Out of those 90 seconds, _____ – _____ percent of that interaction is based on the color of the product or the brand.

10. According to color psychology, different colors have different effects on the moods and behaviors of consumers. They can either calm them ___________ or increase their _______________.

11. In a study at the Cardiff Business School in the UK, it was observed that whether a color works for a brand or not depends on whether the _______________ is deemed _______________________ for that particular brand according to the industry or niche it belongs to.

12. What is A/B testing?
    a. split testing
    b. a marketing technique
    c. a performance test
    d. all of the above

13. What does CTA stand for? _______________

____

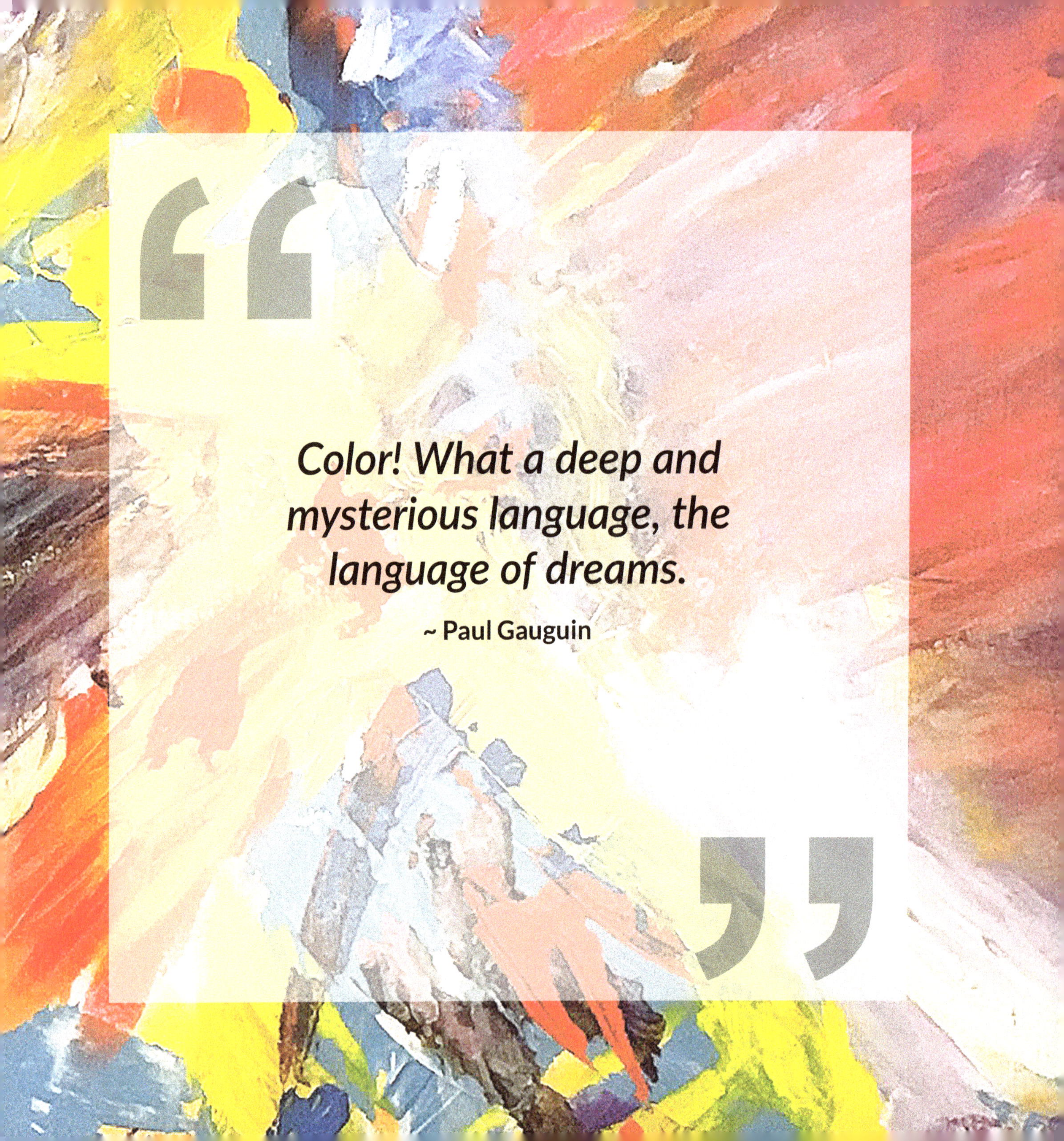

Color! What a deep and mysterious language, the language of dreams.

~ Paul Gauguin

UNDERSTANDING THE MEANING OF COLOR

[APPENDIX]

Answer Key

Part 1 Answers *(Test on page 38)*

1. What are the three primary colors (hint: the parents)? Red, Blue, and Yellow

2. Who invented the color wheel (and discovered the rainbow)? Isaac Newton

3. Who (or what) is ROY G. BIV? The rainbow or Red, Orange, Yellow, Green, Blue, Indigo, and Violet

4. What are secondary colors (or children) born from? Primary colors (or parents)

5. Hue is another way of saying color. True or False? True, hue is what you start with before making tints, shades, and tones.

6. What two "personalities" of color divide the color wheel in half? Warm/Active and Cool/Passive

7. Tertiary colors can be another way of saying intermediate colors. In this book tertiary colors are made from two secondary colors. True or False? True, but the Internet will tell you a different story

8. What can be added to a color to make it a shade of the hue? Black

9. What are the three types of colors on the color wheel? (hint: parents, children, and grandchildren) Primary, secondary, and intermediate (sometimes called tertiary)

10. How are intermediate colors made? By one primary and one secondary color

11. If I add White to a color, I'm making a tint of that color.

12. A color scheme void of color, or desaturated using shades, tint, and tones is called Achromatic.

13. What color scheme is used in this image?

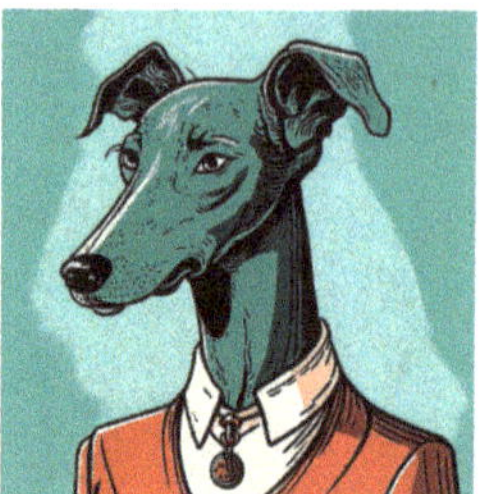

Complementary: Red and Green

14. What color scheme is used in this image?

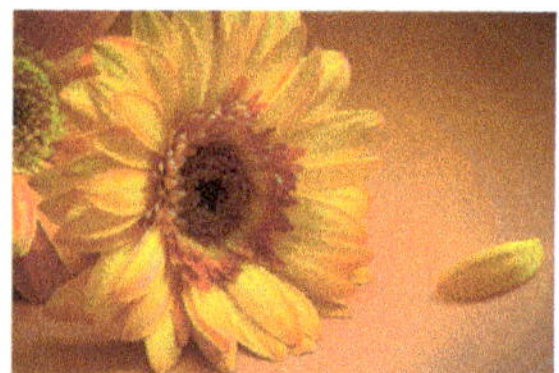

Analogous: Orange, Vermilion, and Red

15. If I was obsessed with a color and wanted to build my color palette with shades, tints and tones of that color, what scheme would I use? Monochromatic

16. Which color scheme forms an equilateral triangle on the color wheel? Triadic

17. The Achromatic color scheme consists of three colors that are side-by-side on the color wheel. True or False? False, it's analogous.

18. A color scheme made up of two complementary pairs of colors is called Tetradic

19. A spit complementary scheme consists of two colors on one side of the color wheel and one color on the other side of the color wheel. True or False? True

Part 2 Answers (Test on page 56)

1. RGB and CMYK are what's known as Color spaces.

2. What color system uses lightwaves to absorb or reflect light? Subtractive

3. In the additive color system all lights shining at once, cause what color to be revealed? White __

4. CMYK and HEX are part of the subtractive color system. True or False? False, HEX is not a part of the subtractive system

5. The RGB color space is used to project colored lights through screens and are a part of the additive color system.

6. What does CMYK stand for? Cyan, Magenta, Yellow, and key (or Black)

7. The secondary colors in CMYK are the same as the primary colors in RGB and vice versa. True or False? True

8. The Pantone® Matching System or PMS is part of the subtractive color system and is best to use as spot color in printing or promotional products such as t-shirts, pens, and mugs which only use one or two colors.

9. What color does #000 make? Black

10. What is the total number of each color value in the RGB color space? 256 because 0 counts as a number and it goes from 0 to 255

11. What CMYK printing process does this illustration represent? Offset printing process

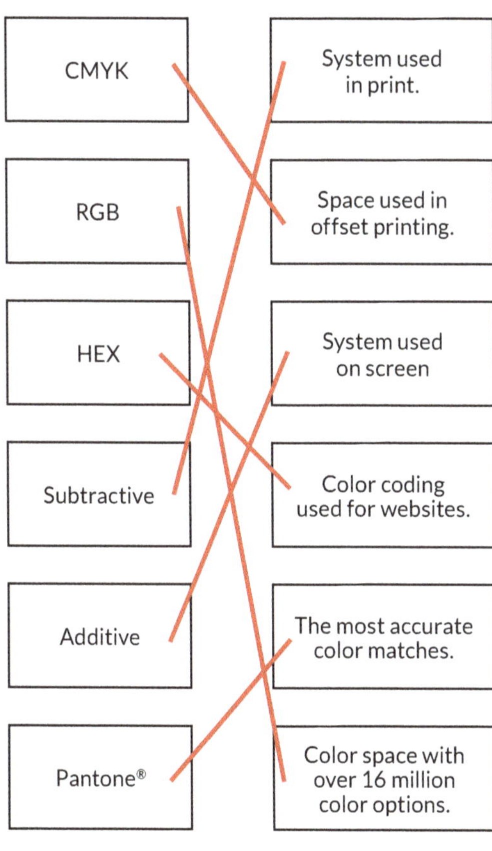

12. Additive and subtractive are the only two color systems. True or False? False

13. Colors in the RGB color space are reduced to combinations of number from 0-9 and letters from A to F to represent the intensity of the three colors, Red, Green, and Blue.

14. PMS stands for Pantone® Matching System

15. Match the words or acronyms on the left with the description that best matches it on the right.

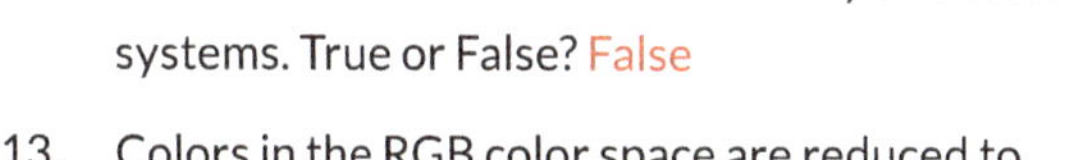

Part 3 Answers *(Test on page 110)*

1. Colors can have both positive and negative effects on consumers, but there are some factors that could come into play like culture. Name 3 other factors:
   geographical locations, demographics, perception, personal preference, experiences from the past, gender, to name a few

2. People can develop a preference or a dislike for a color based on emotional experiences they've had with that particular color in their past. True or False? True.

3. According to Faber Birren's study, using cool/passive colors like Green or Blue causes people to underestimate the passage of time while using warm/active colors like Red and Yellow makes them overestimate the passage of time.

4. The isolation effect is when something stands out like a sore thumb and will likely soon be forgotten. True or False? False

5. What is the most popular brand color? Blue

6. The following is a table of effect symbols. Please fill out the table according to the headings of each column. Under the Effects column name at least two effects associated with the symbol; then, tell whether it is a positive or negative effect under the Pos/Neg? column; and lastly, name one or more colors that can have that effect.

Symbol	Effects	Pos/Neg?	Color(s)
	Conservative, Intelligent, Nostalgic, Professional, Seriousness, Traditional, Wisdom	Pos	Gray
	Eccentricity, Oddity, Quirky, Somberness, Twisted	Neg	Purple
	Cheapness, Immaturity, Frivolity, Simple-minded	Neg	Orange, Pink, Purple
	Elitism, Exclusivity, High Maintenance, Isolation, Oppression	Neg	Purple

Symbol	Effects	Pos/Neg?	Color(s)
	Alive, Down to Earth, Freshness, Growth, Health, Natural, Wellness, Vitality, Earthiness	Pos	Green, Brown
	Faithful, Femininity, Love, Passionate, Romance, Sensitivity, Trusting, Vulnerability	Pos	Pink
	Comfort, Encouragement, Positivity, Warmth	Pos	Yellow, Orange
	Simplicity Minimalism	Pos	Gray

7. Of all the brands in Brandsville, which one's brand color(s) were chosen because the CEO is color blind? Facebook

8. Which brand in Brandsville probably chose their color(s) to encourage fast turnover, satisfied customers, and a cravable product? McDonalds

9. According to Professor Singh's study, it takes around 90 seconds for a consumer to create an opinion about a product. Out of those 90 seconds, 60–90 percent of that interaction is based on the color of the product or the brand.

10. According to color psychology, different colors have different effects on the moods and behaviors of consumers. They can either calm them down or increase their anxiety.

11. In a study at the Cardiff Business School in the UK, it was observed that whether a color works for a brand or not depends on whether the color is deemed appropriate for that particular brand according to the industry or niche it belongs to.

12. What is A/B testing?
    a. split testing   c. a performance test
    b. a marketing technique   d. all of the above

13. What does CTA stand for? Call-to-Action

Glossary

A/B Testing: A marketing technique that compares two versions of a web page or application to see which performs better, also known as split testing.

Active Colors: Active colors are the same as warm colors that evoke warmth and energy (i.e. Reds, Oranges, and Yellows).

Additive Color System: The process of creating colors by combining different intensities of light. In additive color mixing, combining all three primary colors (Red, Green, and Blue) at full intensity produces White light.

Analogous Colors: Colors that are adjacent to each other on the color wheel.

Brand Colors: Brand colors specified using Pantone numbers, CMYK, RGB, and HEX to ensure that their logos and promotional materials maintain consistent colors across various media.

Brand Guidelines: A set of rules and standards that govern the usage and application of a brand's visual identity.

Brand Identity: The visual and emotional representation of a brand. It encompasses the brand's logo, colors, typography, imagery, and overall brand aesthetic that communicates its values and personality.

Brand Loyalty: The tendency of consumers to buy the same brand of product over and over again rather than trust competing brands.

Brand Mark: A distinctive visual element used to identify a brand, such as a symbol or icon.

Brand Personality: The human characteristics and traits associated with a brand.

Brand Positioning: The unique space and perception a brand occupies in the minds of consumers.

Chromotherapy: The use of specific colors to balance and enhance the body's energy centers or chakras.

CMYK Color Space: Stands for Cyan, Magenta, Yellow, and Black (key). It is a color model used in subtractive color mixing, commonly used in color printing. The "K" stands for Black to improve depth and clarity in printed images.

Color Association: The psychological connections and meanings people attribute to certain colors.

Color Blindness: A visual impairment that affects the perception of certain colors or color combinations.

Color Contrast: The difference in value, saturation, or hue between elements of color in a design. The higher the contrast, the bigger the difference.

Color Effects: The emotional and psychological impact that colors can have on individuals.

Color Harmony: The pleasing arrangement and combination of colors in a design.

Color Model: A mathematical model describing the way colors can be represented as tuples of numbers, typically in three or four dimensions. RGB is a common color model in the additive system.

Color Perception: The way individuals interpret and respond to different colors.

Color Preferences: The individual or collective preferences for certain colors based on personal experiences and cultural influences.

Color Psychology: The study of how colors can influence human emotions, moods, and behavior.

Color Scheme: A planned combination of colors used in a design or composition.

Color Symbolism: The use of colors to convey specific meanings or associations.

Color Temperature: The perceived warmth or coolness of a color.

Color Theory: The study and understanding of how colors interact, blend, and harmonize with each other to create visual effects and convey meaning.

Color Therapy: The use of colors to promote physical, mental, and emotional well-being.

Color Wheel: A circular representation of colors that shows their relationships and organization.

Competitive Analysis: Assessing the strengths and weaknesses of competitors to identify opportunities and differentiate a brand.

Complementary Colors: Colors that are opposite each other on the color wheel.

Complementary Colors: Colors that are opposite each other on the color wheel. When placed together, they create strong contrast and enhance each other's intensity.

Composition: The arrangement and organization of visual elements within a design. It involves the consideration of balance, contrast, spacing, and overall visual harmony.

Contrast: The difference between elements in a design, such as color, size, or shape. Contrast helps create visual interest, hierarchy, and emphasis.

Cool Colors: Colors that evoke a sense of coolness and tranquility. They include Blues, Greens, and Purples and are associated with calmness, relaxation, and serenity.

CTA: Call-to-action. A sentence, phrase, or button used in advertising channels (i.e. emails, websites, direct mail) to encourage action in consumers.

Cultural Color Symbolism: The significance and meaning of colors within specific cultures or societies.

HEX Color System: The hexadecimal color system is a series of codes that consists of six digits, divided into three pairs. Each pair represents the intensity of one of the RGB components—Red, Green, and Blue. The hexadecimal color system is commonly used for specifying colors on the web.

Hue: The property of a color that distinguishes it from other colors. It refers to a specific color such as Red, Blue, or Yellow, but does not have to be a color that exists on the color wheel.

Intermediate Colors: Colors formed by mixing a primary color with an adjacent secondary color on the color wheel. Examples include Yellow-Green, Blue-Violet, and Red-Orange. These are also referred to as Tertiary Colors.

Logo: A graphic symbol or emblem that represents a brand or organization. It serves as a visual identifier and helps establish brand recognition and recall.

Market Research: The process of gathering and analyzing data to understand consumer behavior, preferences, and market trends.

Monochromatic Colors: A color scheme that uses variations of a single color by adjusting its value or saturation.

Negative Space: Also known as white space, it refers to the empty or blank areas surrounding and between design elements. It provides breathing room, enhances readability, and contributes to the overall balance of a design.

Pantone® Matching System: A standardized color reproduction system widely used in the printing and graphic design industry. It allows designers, printers, and manufacturers to match colors accurately by referring to a standardized color guide.

Passive Colors: Passive colors are the same as cool colors that evoke coolness and tranquility (i.e., Blues, Greens, and Purples).

PMS: Refers to the Pantone® Matching System.

Primary Colors: The three basic colors on the color wheel, namely Red, Blue, and Yellow, from which all other colors can be derived. They cannot be created by mixing other colors. In the subtractive color system, Cyan, Magenta, and Yellow are the primary colors, and in the additive color system the primary colors are Red, Green, and Blue.

Raster: a type of digital image also known as a bitmap that uses tiny rectangular colored pixels, or picture elements, arranged in a grid formation to represent an image. These elements are a fixed size based on resolution. Therefore, scaling can cause pixel distortion.

RGB Color Space: RGB stands for Red, Green, Blue. It is a color model used in additive color mixing, commonly used in electronic displays such as computer monitors, television screens, and cameras.

Saturation: The intensity or purity of a color. Highly saturated colors appear vivid and vibrant, while desaturated colors appear muted or washed out.

Secondary Colors: Colors created by mixing two primary colors together. They include Orange (Red and Yellow), Green (Yellow and Blue), and Purple (Blue and Red).

Split-Complementary Colors: A color scheme that uses a base color and two colors adjacent to its complementary color.

Spot Colors: Pantone colors are often referred to as "spot colors" because they are pre-mixed inks applied as individual, distinct colors. This is in contrast to process colors (CMYK), which are created by blending different percentages of Cyan, Magenta, Yellow, and Black inks.

Subtractive Color System: The process of creating colors by subtracting specific wavelengths of light. In subtractive color mixing, combining all three primary colors (Cyan, Magenta, and Yellow) at full intensity produces Black.

Tagline: A memorable phrase or slogan that captures the essence of a brand.

Target Audience: The specific group of people that a brand aims to reach and engage.

Tertiary Colors: Colors formed by mixing two secondary colors on the color wheel, making rich colors like Olive (Green and Orange), Slate (Orange and Purple), and Burnt Sienna (Purple and Green) that don't necessarily live on the color wheel. Tertiary can be interpreted as third in importance. Therefore it can also refer to intermediate colors, which are mixed using a primary color and an adjacent secondary color on the color wheel.

Tetradic Colors: A color scheme that uses two sets of complementary colors.

Triadic Colors: A color scheme that uses three colors that are evenly spaced on the color wheel.

Typography: The style, arrangement, and appearance of text. It includes the selection of fonts, sizes, spacing, and formatting to create visually appealing and legible text.

Unique Selling Proposition (USP): The distinctive feature or benefit that sets a brand apart from competitors.

Value: The lightness or darkness of a color. It refers to how much White or Black is mixed with a hue. A high value indicates a lighter color, while a low value indicates a darker color.

Vector: a type of digital image also know as "object-oriented" that is made up of lines, curves, points, and shapes that are based on mathematical formulas. Unlike raster, these files can be scaled without loss of quality.

Visual Identity: The visual elements that comprise a brand's overall identity, including the logo, colors, typography, imagery, and design elements. It ensures consistency and recognition across various brand touchpoints.

Warm Colors: Colors that evoke warmth and energy. They include Reds, Oranges, and Yellows and are associated with excitement, passion, and vitality.

Color Palette Resources

Adobe Color (color.adobe.com/) An easy-to-use, web-based tool for creating color schemes. You can also explore color trends and generate color palettes using your favorite images.

Colorhunt (colorhunt.co/) A community platform—like social media for colors—used to discover and share color palettes created by members of the community.

Coolors (coolors.co/) A cool color scheme generator that helps you create color palettes quickly. You can also save and share them.

Design Seeds (www.design-seeds.com/) This is an informative website that showcases color palettes inspired by images from nature, fashion, and everyday life.

Paletton (paletton.com/) A fun, interactive color scheme designer based on color theory principles.

Color Conversion Tools

Rapid Tables (www.rapidtables.com/convert/color/) Offers a collection of color conversion calculators for not just RGB, HEX, and CMYK color spaces but also HSL, HSV, and XYZ color spaces. I told you there were other ones out there.

Studio Red (www.studiored.com/rgb-hex-to-pantone-color-converter/) Once you've figured out the RGB or HEX number, you can use this converter to determine if there is a Pantone® match. This converter will give you several options labeled with the "distance" to show how close to the color it is. Zero being the closest. It's hard to know for sure without a Pantone® book or swatch. Remember that what you are seeing on the screen is in the RGB color space, and may be somewhat distorted.

Pantone® www.pantone.com/ You can purchase Pantone® swatch books here. Plus, get a lot more information about color trends.

www.ingramcontent.com/pod-product-compliance
Lightning Source LLC
Chambersburg PA
CBHW041816130726
48010CB00004BA/181